THE POSITIVE PRINCIPLE TODAY

NORMAN VINCENT PEALE

A FIRESIDE BOOK
Published by Simon & Schuster
New York   London   Toronto   Sydney

Marianne Jewell Memorial Library
Baker College of Muskegon
Muskegon, Michigan 49442

FIRESIDE
Rockefeller Center
1230 Avenue of the Americas
New York, NY 10020

First Fireside Edition 2003

FIRESIDE and colophon are registered trademarks
of Simon & Schuster, Inc.

For information regarding special discounts for bulk purchases,
please contact Simon & Schuster Special Sales at 1-800-456-6798
or business@simonandschuster.com

Manufactured in the United States of America

10 9 8 7 6 5 4 3 2

Library of Congress Cataloging-in-Publication Data
Peale, Norman Vincent.
    Positive principle today/Norman Vincent Peale.—1st Fireside ed.
      p.   cm.
    1. Success—Religious aspects—Christianity. I. Title.
    BJ1611.2.P4   2003   248.4—dc21   2002042658

We acknowledge with thanks permission to use the following material:
Barefoot to America by Legson Kayira, copyright © April 1964,
Guideposts Magazine, Carmel, N.Y. 10512. Used by permission. *My
Flight for Life* by Brian Steed, copyright © February 1973, *Guideposts
Magazine,* Carmel, N.Y. 10512. Used by permission. *I Remember Three
Christmases* by Norman Vincent Peale, copyright © December 1974,
Guideposts Magazine, Carmel, N.Y. 10512. Used by permission. From
"He Keeps Me Singing," copyright 1910. Renewal 1937 Broadman Press.
All rights reserved. Used by permission.

ISBN 0-7432-3489-8

FOREWORD

This book, of course, has a purpose, a definite objective. Let me explain it in the hope that what follows may be meaningful and helpful to you.

For a long time I have caught myself saying to people who are doing well, reaching goals and accomplishing desirable objectives—"Keep it going." To those who were obviously on the right track, I am likely to say in a friendly way—"Keep it going." And to people who seem to be dragging along with only a fragment of the enthusiasm they once had, I find myself encouraging them to remember the positive principle and—"Keep it going."

Then among the hundreds of letters received was a rather special one, as it turned out, for the question it posed led me to an in-depth study and research of the positive principle, and how to keep it going.

The letter read as follows:

Dear Dr. Peale:
    I read as many inspirational and motivational books as I can find, yours among them. They lift me to a higher mental level, and I'm fired with zest and enthusiasm for everything.
    As a result I do much better in my job and certainly I'm a great deal happier. But somehow I cannot hold the inspiration all that long, especially if I run into problems and setbacks. They act as a drain on my high spirits and presently I find myself feeling like a deflated balloon—really down.
    I know you will think I am flighty and superficial,

and perhaps that's true. Yet at the same time I'm genuinely responsive to motivational and inspirational suggestions and teaching. What I want to know is how to keep the positive principle going in the tough experiences which everyone has to face.

You and other writers have the power to activate my mind. Please tell me how to be consistently reactivated; how to have a constant renewal of inspiration sufficient to withstand frustrating situations and depressing moments. What I want to know is how to keep motivation going—always to keep it going! And I'll thank you a lot if you will tell me.

The foregoing letter rather clearly expresses a perennial human problem—that of maintaining inspirational attitudes over the long pull, in dark days as well as in sunny and fortuitous times. The tendency of the mental level to sag or droop is a common problem. How to sustain the positive principle and keep an upbeat mental attitude is a concern to which an inspirational writer should, I believe, address himself.

That is what we mean to do. It is the author's hope that this book will not only inspire and motivate you to think, act and live victoriously, but will also help you always and under whatever circumstances to keep it going, ever stronger and more vitally.

Norman Vincent Peale

INTRODUCTION

What Is the Positive Principle?

There is a deep tendency in human nature to become precisely what we imagine or picture ourselves to be. We tend to equate with our own self-appraisal of either depreciation or appreciation. We ourselves determine either self-limitation or unlimited growth potential.

The negative thinker engages ultimately in a self-destroying process. As he constantly sends out negative thoughts, he activates the world around him negatively. There is a law of attraction, in which like attracts like. Birds of a feather flock together. Thoughts of a kind have a natural affinity. The negative thinker, projecting negative thoughts, tends thereby to draw back to himself negative results. This is a definite and immutable law of mind.

The positive thinker, on the contrary, constantly sends out positive thoughts, together with vital mental images of hope, optimism and creativity. He therefore activates the world around him positively and strongly tends to draw back to himself positive results. This, too, is a basic law of mind action.

But the negative thinker can dramatically improve his outcomes by a thorough revamping of the negative type of thinking hitherto employed. As William James, the noted philosopher-psychologist, suggested, "The greatest discovery of my generation is that human beings can alter their lives by altering their attitudes of mind."

The positive principle is the vital process of mental and spiritual alteration whereby the individual shifts from a concept of self-limitation to that of self-improvement, from deterioration to growth, from failure to accomplishment.

The positive principle is a totality of sound thinking, dealing forthrightly and creatively with the realistic facts of human existence. The positive thinker sees every difficulty and sees them straight. Nor is he abashed by them, nor does he seek an escapist "out" from them. He knows that every problem contains the seeds of its own solution, as the well-known idea expert Stanley Arnold said. He also knows that by the help of God and the release of his own inherent powers, he has what it takes to deal with, handle and solve any problem. Therefore, as a healthy-minded individual, he or she stands up to difficulty fearlessly and confidently. The positive thinker does not react emotionally when in difficulty, recognizing the fact that the human mind cannot function at its best when it is hot or emotionally conditioned. The positive thinker is aware that only when the mind is cool, even cold, and under strong mental control, will it produce those dispassionate, rational and intellectual concepts that lead to sound and viable solutions.

The positive principle is based on the fact that there is always an answer, a right answer, and that positive thinking through a sound intellectual process can always produce that answer.

It is, of course, true that the negative is important in preserving balance. Opposites are involved in the structure of nature. And in the realm of thought the negative has an important function in the consideration of alternatives. But when the negative takes over as the controlling element in the thinking process, the balance swings away from the positive, and negative aspects become dominant.

The negative principle negates. The positive principle creates. The negative principle doubts. The positive principle believes. The negative principle accepts defeat. The positive principle goes for victory.

The positive principle is solidly based on spiritual truth, resting firmly upon those dynamic words "This is the victory that overcometh the world, even our faith."[1]

[1] I John 5:4.

CONTENTS

FIRST
WAY TO KEEP
THE POSITIVE
PRINCIPLE GOING

Organize Your Personality Forces Into Action

Mastering the positive principle and developing the ability to keep it going are basic to successful performance in life. With them you can keep your motivation, your enthusiasm, your inspiration, sustained and replenished—every day, all the way! That is the central message of this book. And supportive of that message, specific techniques are presented, techniques that many persons have found to be highly effective. This book presents a methodology for maintaining the keep-it-going dynamic at high level.

To keep the positive principle going, it is vitally important to maintain an enthusiastic spirit at all times and under whatever conditions. The blows and vicissitudes of personal and business life can, if allowed to do so, draw off enthusiasm and weaken positive attitudes. And since such erosion of spirit is a process of deterioration that every creative person wishes to avoid, it is essential to have a program of reinspiration constantly going for you. Systematic and consistent replenishment of vital spirit is required to keep enthusiasm and motivation at top level.

People can learn to become positive thinkers, and as a result their lives take on new meaning. They are more successful in their jobs. Enthusiasm lifts them to higher

1

levels. Things flow toward them rather than away from them. Even so, unforeseen difficulties may arise, troubles emerge, setbacks occur and the going becomes hard and difficult. It is then that the positive viewpoint must be shored up by a revitalization of inspiration, a renewal of enthusiasm. In this book we mean to lay out simple and workable principles for keeping vital motivation operative regardless of adverse circumstances. It will show how, under varying conditions and situations, personality forces may be organized to produce effective action.

An outstanding positive thinker who stresses the need for "renewable" positive attitudes is Dr. Jan S. Marais of Cape Town, South Africa, Chairman of The Trust Bank. Dr. Marais founded this important banking organization in a modest office on one floor of a business building only a very few years ago. By sound banking principles and innovative procedures he has developed The Trust Bank into one of the great financial institutions of the world. He has employed positive thinking, enthusiasm and top administrative skill in the outstanding success he and his associates have achieved. In a recent letter he says:

> My personal experience and that of my colleagues is that inspiration and motivation are exactly like nutrition. You have to keep on taking it daily, in healthy doses. Otherwise depletion, fatigue depression and lack of ambition and achievement will very soon manifest themselves. Your books, Norman, are mandatory companions of the leadership echelon of The Trust Bank.

This influential business leader, being a wise and understanding man, is aware that the extremely important qualities of inspiration and enthusiasm are not to be

2

taken for granted; they can and often do decline in force and must therefore be replenished daily by a new intake of motivational thinking. It is necessary to activate and reactivate personality forces constantly, and even impel them into action, in order to keep them going, always going. The positive principle must ever be nourished and renourished.

Unlimited Power in Personality

A listener to our radio broadcasts wrote me about an article he had read in a scientific journal which he thought quite fascinating. It stated, so he reports, that an ordinary piece of quartz, electrically stimulated, will vibrate 4,194,302 times a second. That causes one to wonder! If an ordinary piece of quartz responds to stimulus in such extraordinary fashion, what may be expected from the mind and spirit of a human being when personality forces are really activated? The potential, obviously, is unlimited.

For a long time now we have been reading appraisals by various psychologists and scientists in human behavior that the average person uses perhaps only 20 percent of his mental power; even geniuses use but a fraction more. Some even rate the average use of creative power as low as 10 percent. It seems incredible, does it not, that human beings endowed by nature with high potential should employ only one fifth of it in meeting their problems and in building careers in this world? Why is it, one asks, that a piece of quartz, actually a stone, when stimulated can react so incredibly, and at the same time men and women are content to go along acquiescing in a limited human reaction to the opportunities all about them and to the potential within themselves?

It is probably a fact that the average individual accepts a limited concept of himself and his abilities. It never gets through to him that it is possible for this potential to be stepped up; that by creative and positive thinking about himself, he can bring out of the mind an increased quotient of power, force and capacity.

The truth is that there is much more strength and power in the individual than he has ever known or even visualized as a possibility. Remember the insight of the great thinker of antiquity Marcus Aurelius, who said, "Dig within. There lies the well-spring of good: ever dig and it will ever flow."[1] The motivational writer Kermit W. Lueck tells of an unconscious truck driver pinned in the burning cab of an overturned gasoline tank truck. Even strong men in the gathered crowd were unable to open the cab door which had been warped in the crash. Then suddenly an average-sized man appeared, threw off his jacket, grabbed hold of the door handle and with a powerful jerk wrenched it open. Climbing into the cab around which flames raged, he kicked the pedals to free the unconscious driver's feet, arched his slight back against the crushed roof of the cab, and pulled the driver out to safety. Asked later how a man of his build could perform such a feat, he explained that his two children had been burned to death, and that as a result he hated fire with an intense passion.

When he saw this helpless man pinned in a high-octane gasoline truck that could go up in flaming explosion at any moment, his antipathy toward fire brought out of him a strength he did not know he possessed. He only knew that he was going to get that man away from that hated fire. Crisis summoned forth a strength that we call superhuman; but would it not be more accurate to think of it as normal human force hitherto unused? If

[1] *Meditations*, Bk. 7, No. 59.

such strength can emerge under crisis, the fact is that it is present, but untapped, at all times. "Dig within. . . . ever dig and it will ever flow."

GIs Pick Up Jeep in Crisis

Lueck also gives us an account of four GIs who were ambushed on a very narrow road in Vietnam. They leaped into a ditch. Fully aware of their exposed position, suddenly, with common mind, they jumped back to the road and rushed to the jeep, which could not be turned around for lack of space to maneuver. Each man took a wheel and together they lifted the jeep, turned it around quickly, jumped in, and at full speed, through cross fire, headed back to safety. Back at camp, the four men together could not lift one wheel of the jeep off the ground. From what source came the enormous strength of the men at the place of ambush? From within themselves, of course, is the answer.

The question therefore is why, in the problems and difficulties of regular daily existence, do we fail to tap and utilize the amazing powers that are usually produced only under intense crisis? The answer may lie in the fact that we are not sufficiently intense in belief, in faith and in thought. When we develop such intensity, may we not expect that we shall be able to stimulate immense personality forces into action? It seems not too much to believe that we shall release from ourselves capacities we have never actually even dreamed of bringing into play.

Retiree Gets Reactivated

The following incident, which I wrote about in *Senior Power*, a magazine edited and published by Dr. Kenneth P. Berg, happened some years ago in the stock room of

Kroch's and Brentano's bookstore in Chicago, where I was autographing copies of my book *The Power of Positive Thinking*. To my surprise Adolph Kroch, the founder and then recently retired president of the company, came in and began helping me. "Haven't anything else to do," he grumbled. He told me that he tried to stay away from the store, but decades of habit drew him back. Everyone treated him fine, he explained, and his son, Carl, now president, always acted glad to see him. But he was sensitively aware that he was "out of it," didn't really belong anymore. "Guess I'm useless," he declared sadly, "so I'm glad to serve you like a stock room boy."

Then suddenly he asked, "About this positive thinking—why don't you write a book on retirement?"

"Oh, that is not my field. I really am not adequately informed on the subject," I replied. Then I turned the question back on him. "Why don't you write such a book, now that you are retired?"

"Not me," he answered quickly. "I don't write books. I sell them."

We went on for a few minutes in a silence broken only by the stacking up of volumes and the scratching of my pen. "Okay," he said, "perhaps you can take a detached attitude toward the trauma of retirement and express an objective point of view. Give me some advice. If you were in my position, what would you do? What should I do? My health is good and I'm not short on energy and I like to do things that count for something. But here I am on a plateau in my life from which I see no excitement or even usefulness."

"Well, now, look," I replied, "anything I say is bound to be off the cuff, and remember that I'm no expert on the subject of retirement. Yet I do have some knowledge of what others in like position have done, and we can perhaps learn from their experience." I told him that in my opinion it is wise to play down that word "retirement" and to emphasize instead the word and concept "readjustment." Retirement somewhat suggests a drop-out status, a finished state. Readjustment, on the other hand, indicates continuity of activity, though in different capacity and perhaps in entirely new form.

An old Korean man once told me that in his country people think of beginning a new and different life at sixty years; they assume a new birth, gearing themselves for new activity. "I became a resurrected person at sixty," my Korean friend declared, "and have been living as a new man ever since."

Thus there is no reason why anyone in health and strength need acquiesce to the idea so generally and supinely accepted today that an arbitrarily set retirement age must necessarily mean an ipso facto disqualification from new and fresh forms of useful activity. No person, at any age, needs to remain on an uninspiring level of accomplishment.

Therefore I suggested to this unhappy retired executive that he practice the principle of adaptability—say good-bye to his old business, sell his home and move to a different section of the country. See himself once again as he was at the start, an immigrant boy arriving in a new land and looking for opportunities.

"As soon as you get settled in your new home, join a church and tell the minister you want to help him; get in there and get involved. Then hunt up a political club and say you want to be an active worker. Get into a service club and work on its committees. Join the Chamber of Commerce and become a leader. Go all out and you'll get outside yourself. And," I added, "forget all about this bookstore except for your pension check. Practice the spiritual principle suggested in the words 'forgetting those things which are behind, and reaching forth unto those things which are before. . . .' "[2]

There was, of course, nothing unique about this advice, but the result was unique in that the erstwhile book dealer took the advice seriously and acted upon it. And how!

In the small West Coast city where he settled, he became a real estate dealer, a banker, a service club leader, chairman of the local hospital board and head of the Chamber of Commerce. As one local man put it, "Whence came this young-old Lochinvar—this revitalized ball of fire?" And he was still going strong twenty years later. Practically the only time he returned to the old home city was for the funeral of some contemporary who acquiesced in retirement and became a dropout: mentally, physically and spiritually. Mr. Kroch practiced positive thinking in retirement, with positive results. He discovered that he was not through, far from it. He tapped some inner resources never before discovered and brought forth extra capacities he did not know he possessed. By stimulating the forces of his personality into revitalized action he created a new and exciting life. The enthusiasms and motivations which had made him a leader in business and community were reemployed in the retired situation. He became an inspiring example of how to keep the positive principle going, and vigorously.

Handling the IFs in Life

It is very important to be on top of life's circumstances, always in control, for human existence can and often

[2]Philippians 3:13.

does follow an uncertain and variable pattern. It can turn on you, trip you up, hit you hard, throw the book at you—unless it is managed and controlled. Nevertheless, existence on earth is, I believe, intended to be *for* us rather than against us. If everyone followed the purposes of the Creator, the general thrust of life would be in our favor, though not without some hard going at times, for the Great Architect of the Universe did not eliminate pain and struggle and difficulty. He knew these to be for our good in the development of a strong person, and that objective just has to be basic to His purpose in creating man and woman in the first place. No person can become strong without struggle, without the effort of pitting himself against trouble and hardship. And to meet and deal with life creatively we will always need to be alert and thoughtful and to think in a positive manner, constantly rallying personality forces into effective and desirable action. We must be aware of and prepared for life's variable, unpredictable and uncertain nature, caused basically by that same mix of qualities in ourselves.

I happened to notice one day that the word "life"—*l-i-f-e*—significantly has an *if* at its center. The central two letters of the four-letter word representing existence form a concept of uncertainty which is designated by *if*. And the potency of *if* is every day underscored in the language of many persons. "If I do this," "If I do that," "If this happens," "If that happens," "If only I had not said [or done] that." So it goes, on and on and still on, the repetitive *if* element. Can it be a fact that half of life is an *if* even as it constitutes half of the word which stands for existence on earth? If so, or whatever proportion the *if* factor represents, it is all the more reason why we must assume a firmer control of those uncertainties, the *ifs*, and make them into certainties, thereby contributing to, rather than detracting from, our best potential.

Strange Thing Happens

On a speaking trip in the West I met Jeff, a thirty-five-year-old man who had been, as he put it, "in the grip of a failure pattern for some time." It appeared that hardly anything was going right, and that fact was getting to him to such an extent that he was admitting defeat and failure. He had developed into a negative "if only" man, constantly bemoaning, "If only I had not done that stupid thing," "If that guy had only given me a break"; one dismal *if* after another. His career, he had come to admit, had become dependent upon whims and variables, and he had practically no sense of control over the circumstances, to his mind all negative, which seemed to gang up on him.

Some time before our meeting Jeff was sitting, glum and desultory, in his motel room, listening to a late-night television show originating in New York and on which I happened to appear as a guest. The interviewer took as the subject of our discussion the question of how people who are not making it on their jobs can get a new grip on themselves and start strong motivations going. I developed the concept that one can impel his personality powers into action by intense desire, intense belief and intense prayer, using the word "intense" to differentiate these factors from the usual bland attitudes of so many. I recall quoting from James Russell Lowell:

> I, that still pray at morning and at eve, . . .
> Thrice in my life perhaps have truly prayed,
> Thrice, stirred below my conscious self, have felt
> That perfect disenthralment which is God. . . .

We had a stimulating give-and-take on the TV show about the meaning of that concept and agreed that by thrusting beneath the surface of the mind and into the area of faith by intense and in-depth desire, a person could reorganize personality forces that had been floundering and reducing him to ineffectiveness.

Two thousand miles away, Jeff told me, he was listening to this TV show, which certainly had no reputation of being dedicated generally to God- or prayer-talk. Suddenly he had a remarkable experience of deep insight. In a flash he became aware that in this intense prayer-faith formula lay the correction of his failure pattern. Acting at once upon the suggestions which were made on the air, he began a prayer-faith program. Continuing it daily, he found God like never before —like he never thought possible. One result was that his negative *if* emphasis began to give way to the positive *how* principle. Rather than futilely mumbling *ifs*, he began instead to stress "How can it be done?" "How can I do it better?" "How can I really get going?" Result—a dramatic reorganization of his personality forces. Moreover, along with this personality reconstruction, Jeff became infused with such strong motivation that discouragements gradually lessened and over a period of time he developed a new sense of control over difficulties. This man definitely learned the secret of keeping it going. He got aboard the positive principle and went on successfully from there.

Amazing Personality Forces

No doubt there are those who, for one reason or another, either doubt or resist the assertion that as persons they possess forces that are beyond the average abilities they have been able to develop. "There just isn't all that in me despite your flattering appraisal of my worth. I'm just a normal, average person." To that I must answer, "Maybe average, but hardly normal, for the word 'normal' refers to 'norm,' and that in turn stands for a level of attainment that is open to our determination. It is hardly normal to be less than your best, for if less than best is normal, or the norm of achievement, we would scarcely ever be activated by a discontent with ourselves as we are. And thus progress would be stymied."

To settle for self-limitation is to lock yourself up within yourself and therefore to deny to yourself the God-given opportunity for growth. So I urge you to avoid that "I'm an average person" expression of self-depreciation. Instead, get a new view of your personality, which presupposes greater abilities than you have ever before visualized. Move your idea of your norm up to higher levels, as the bar is moved from one level to another in a track meet for high jumpers or pole vaulters. Always you can go higher, for within yourself you are greater than you think. Believe that, for it is a fact—a great, big, truthful, wonderful fact. It is the positive principle in action.

The famous Olympic champion Bob Richards, who is also a popular and highly respected motivational speaker and writer, has pointed out[3] that all Olympic champions are people who believe in themselves and therefore in that extra power built into personality. Some have even specified to the split second how they are going to do in a race. Mark Spitz said he would win seven gold medals. On the first try he won only two, but in his last competition he did win the visualized seven. He knew he was capable of seven if he used his potential. Such champions prove the fact that there is a greater personality force that can, under appropriate circumstances, be summoned into magnificent action.

Richards tells of teaching a Sunday School class and

[3]"How to Get What You Deserve—The Best." *Success Unlimited.*

telling the students about the qualities that go into making champion athletes. He was interrupted by a very fat little girl with thick bifocals who kept jumping up and down saying she was going to be the greatest woman tennis player in the world. This little girl was Billie Jean Moffitt, later Billie Jean King, perhaps the greatest woman tennis player in the world, and perhaps we would not be amiss to drop the qualifying word "woman." She responded with powerful motivation and belief to the idea of super-faculties within that could be mustered into action.

Bob Richards declares in his article that if you will write on a card what you intend to be in life, making it specific, and keep that card for constant reference and embed that goal deeply in your mind for a period of two years, you will become what you said you would achieve. He asserts that he can demonstrate this truth from athletic history. Bill Vandervoort, prominent sportswriter, supports the positive concept of being the best you can be in quoting the football coach Woody Hayes, of Ohio State University, famous for great teams:

> Ohio State's Woody Hayes sounded like Norman Vincent Peale Saturday following the Buckeyes' 32–7 romp over North Carolina.
>
> Peale, the noted theologian, has no better exponent of his "power of positive thinking" than Big Buck. A Chicago writer asked Hayes in the locker-room afterwards how he continued to attract top players.
>
> "It's very simple," replied Woody. "We recruit and coach on a positive basis. We seek the quality, the best kids. I couldn't get along with any other kind. Then we set high standards, we challenge them to be better than they think they can be.
>
> "Once they find out how they can be better, they respond to you, respect you. I get sick and tired of the

way our society talks down to everyone. I believe in reaching the best in the boy."[4]

Someone sent me a newspaper clipping in which a woman tells of her remarkable experience with the visualization or mental image principle in making the best things happen:

> Twelve years ago, Helen Hadsell's husband wanted an outboard motor that was the top prize in a contest.
> She concentrated, wrote a 25-word entry, and won it.
> Her daughter wanted a bicycle. A little concentration on mother's part and the daughter had her bike.
> The family wanted to go to Europe. Mom found a contest offering a European vacation prize, concentrated, and off they went. They returned to Europe two more times the same way.
> Thirty-three times Mrs. Hadsell concentrated on winning contest prizes, and 33 times she won, including the $50,000 house that was the top prize in a contest at the New York World's Fair in 1964.
> "There were 2 million entries in the house contest," said Mrs. Hadsell. "I did what I had done in every other contest: I simply pictured myself owning that house.
> "I have won everything by applying the principle of Dr. Norman Vincent Peale's book, 'The Power of Positive Thinking.' I picked up the book at a newsstand 12 years ago and read it.
> "What he was saying is if you *know* what you want, and you hang in there long enough and strong enough, you'll get what you want. It is simply constructive thinking. I got from Dr. Peale's book the endless possibilities that are available from positive thinking. I applied that to contests, and I won.
> "The secret," she said, "is always stressing the end result, knowing you have what it is you want. If I was vying for a prize, I visualized a check, right there in my hand."[5]

[4]Dayton *Daily News.*
[5]Indianapolis *News.*

We may comment that Mrs. Hadsell made a valid principle operationally effective, but obviously she added the force of a facile and innovative mind. The point of the matter is that creative attitudes can create wonders. That which we intensely image can and often does actualize in fact.

The Magic of Believing

In my opinion, one of the few greatest inspirational and motivational books ever written in the United States is *The Magic of Believing*, by Claude Bristol. I knew Mr. Bristol personally and through the years was profoundly affected by the dynamic spirit of this man's mind and writings. He truly believed in the spiritual principle "If thou canst believe, all things are possible to him that believeth."[6]

Claude Bristol in his book deals with the immense powers of the mind when activated by strong belief freed of stultifying doubt. In compelling illustration after illustration he documents the magic of believing in the varied lives of the failures turned into successes who march triumphantly across the pages of his book. He, too, knew the astonishing power of the mind when committed to the realization of a specified goal. One of the techniques for realization which he often suggested is to take five 3″ by 5″ cards, and on one of them write succinctly but in explicit detail what you want, deeply want with all your mind and heart. Duplicate this on the other four cards. Then put one in your wallet or purse, another over your shaving or dressing table mirror, one over the kitchen sink, one on your car's instrument panel and the fifth on your desk. Look intently at the card every day, meanwhile printing the mental image firmly in consciousness. Visualize your objective or goal,

[6]Mark 9:23.

which is now in the process of being actualized. That this method works can be attested to by the thousands of grateful readers and practitioners of *The Magic of Believing*. This book is one of the great expositions of the positive principle.

Saw Himself as Great Editor

A highly successful friend of mine always credited the success he achieved as one of America's greatest newspaper publishers to Orison Swett Marden, a much earlier but profoundly influential motivational writer. This friend and close associate for many years was the late Roger Ferger, publisher and editor of the Cincinnati *Enquirer*, one of the outstanding newspapers in the nation. Mr. Ferger was a notably strong and capable leader in community affairs and was greatly respected for his high order of intelligence.

One day as Mr. Ferger and I were returning to the *Enquirer* office after a luncheon together at the Queen City Club, of which he was president, we stopped in front of the newspaper building. I asked him, "Roger, tell me, just how did you become editor and publisher of the Cincinnati *Enquirer*?"

He said, "Many years ago as a young boy I stood on this very spot and, looking into that window, saw a man sitting at a desk. He was the editor and publisher of this paper. Right then and there I had a vision of myself sitting in his place, bearing his title and carrying forward his work. I suddenly wanted to be editor and publisher. I visualized myself as in that position and from that moment forward worked diligently to attain that goal. I believed, I believed, I believed, and became a practitioner of the power of positive thinking which you have so long been advocating and teaching."

He then took from his wallet a yellowed and somewhat tattered clipping from the writings of Orison Swett Marden, and standing on the sidewalk, traffic roaring by, he read it to me. I think I shall always remember the look of enthusiastic faith which was reflected on his countenance as he spoke words which had motivated him as a young boy and had continued to stir his personality forces into action throughout a notably successful life. And these are the dynamic words which started him and which helped him always to keep it going: "A man who is self-reliant, positive, optimistic, and undertakes his work with the assurance of success magnetizes his condition. He draws to himself the creative powers of the universe."

I related this story in less detail some years ago when I wrote *The Power of Positive Thinking*, and re-emphasize it here for the reason that in the thousands of letters received since publication of that book, many have referred gratefully to the activation of their own personality force by Mr. Ferger's experience.

Maybe the objection will be made that this was an unusually gifted man, that he would have attained successful outcomes without recourse to such believing and reactivating principles. May I then give you, in concluding this chapter, the experience of another man mentioned in that same book whose story has been the spark that lifted countless others out of failure and set them on the road to making something extra good of their lives?

I reprint a letter received a few years ago from a man telling how the positive principle dramatically changed his father's business experience, and his life in general. He wrote as follows:

> My father was a traveling salesman. One time he sold furniture, another time hardware, sometimes it was leather goods. He changed his line every year.

17

I would hear him telling Mother that this was his last trip in stationery or in bed lamps or whatever he was selling at the moment. Next year everything would be different; we would be on Easy Street; he had a chance to go with a firm that had a product that sold itself. It was always the same. My father never had a product that sold. He was always tense, always afraid of himself, always whistling in the dark.

Then one day a fellow-salesman gave Father a copy of a little three-sentence prayer. He was told to repeat it just before calling on a customer. Father tried it and the results were almost miraculous. He sold 85 percent of all calls during the first week, and every week thereafter the results were wonderful. Some weeks the percentage ran as high as 95 percent, and Father had 16 weeks in which he sold every customer called on.

Father gave this prayer to several other salesmen, and in each case it brought astounding results. The prayer Father used is as follows:

> "I believe I am always divinely guided.
> I believe I will always take the right turn of the road.
> I believe God will always make a way where there is no way."

A simple prayer, I grant you, but as a thought and action stimulator it is invested with rare power. Unconsciously this hitherto desultory salesman had employed the amazing resources of faith in God, the belief in guidance, and the power of visualization and affirmation. As a result his personality underwent dramatic change. The power within him, so long held in abeyance, surged forth in an incredible stream of effective action. He became literally a new man, remade and vital. His personality forces, so long dormant, were released into action, and not merely on a temporary basis. So great were the newly activated powers that they constantly replenished themselves. Hence, as Dr. Marais said at the opening of this chapter, "Inspiration and motivation are exactly like nutrition. You have to keep on taking it daily, in healthy doses. Otherwise depletion, fatigue, depression and lack of ambition and achievement will very soon manifest themselves."

This salesman, by use of that simple but powerful affirmative and visualized spiritual principle, took in vitalized thought food and his entire life was changed. He thereafter possessed a new and vigorous power to keep it going.

And now here is the way personality forces are released into action:

1. Motivation is like nutrition. It must be taken daily and in healthy doses to keep it going.
2. There is much more power in personality than has ever been used; release it.
3. Life has an *if* at the center of the word and of our existence as well. Assume control of those variable and uncertain *ifs*.
4. Believe in and accept and affirm the powerful personality force inherent within you.
5. Practice the amazingly creative magic of believing.
6. "See" yourself, "image" yourself as what you want to be; then be just that.
7. Believe that the miracle of change is always possible—for you. Indeed, believe it is even *now* taking place.
8. Make a new and total commitment to the positive principle and master the skill of keeping it going.

SECOND
WAY TO KEEP
THE POSITIVE
PRINCIPLE GOING

Take a New Look at That Word "Impossible"

The positive principle will help you get out of trouble and stay out thereafter. Let me tell you a story about Fred and Jennifer, who were in trouble—real trouble. They were heavily in debt and the small clothing shop they operated showed every ominous sign of failing.

It was a time of acute financial depression and their city had been hit hard. Indeed, businesses were closing all around them. It appeared as if their turn to fold would not be long in coming. The number of unpaid accounts on their books totaled a dangerously high figure. So little money was coming in that the bills from their suppliers could not be paid unless something happened, and quickly.

One morning Fred and Jennifer were sitting glumly in their little office going over their bills and unpaid accounts. It all seemed completely futile. No patrons at all were in the shop, which had been allowed to run down into shabby appearance.

Then something quite unexpected but very exciting happened. A scientist, prominent in chemical research and a friend of the couple, was walking along a street not far away. Some impulse told him to go around to see Fred and Jennifer. He could not shake off the impression that it was urgently important for him to make this call.

How the Impossible Turned Into Possibles

The scientist friend found the young couple in a state of mind bordering on despair mixed with panic. To his quite unnecessary question, "How's business?" Fred took a sheet of paper and printed on it in large letters the word IMPOSSIBLE and shoved it in front of their friend, a great human being named Dr. Alfred E. Cliffe. He studied the graphic word, then said thoughtfully, "Let's take a look at that word, 'impossible.' Just see what can be done with it if you don't let it overwhelm you." So saying, he took a big black pencil and drew two lines, one through the I, the other through the M, so that now it looked like this: IMPOSSIBLE. The word POSSIBLE, freed of the IM, stood out strong and clear. "Nothing," he said, "nothing is impossible if you do not think impossible. So what do you say? Let's start seeing only possibles. Let's apply the positive principle to your situation."

Al Cliffe picked up the top invoice from the stack of bills ready to be sent to their accounts. "John Abbott," he read. "What do you know about Mr. Abbott? Has he a wife and children? Wonder how he is getting along in his own business?"

"How should I know?" growled Fred. "He's just a customer and a slow-paying one at that."

"Tell you what," said Al, "look him up in the telephone directory. Give him a call and just ask in a friendly sort of way how things are. And do it now."

Grudgingly Fred did as directed and had a conversation that must have been pleasing judging by the first smile he had come up with. "He seemed pleased," he reported, "and quite surprised at my interest. He asked how we were doing and when I told him we were having a time collecting and paying bills he said he was in the same fix and added that he hadn't forgotten us, though I assured him that was not the reason for my call."

Then Al Cliffe did a strange thing. He asked Fred and Jennifer to join him in placing their right hands on that stack of outgoing bills. He prayed aloud for all the persons represented in that pile of bills, not for them to pay up, but that each of them would be blessed according to his own particular problems.

"Now, let's have an idea session," he suggested. "Got enough money for a can of paint?"

"Yeah, we're not all that low," grumbled Fred.

"Okay, get busy and paint the interior of the store shiny white. Then wash those showcases and windows until they glisten. Get some new light bulbs in those overhead fixtures. Most of all, get a smile on your faces and stay in the shop expecting business. When people start coming, greet them with real friendliness. Keep thinking in terms of the possibles. Skip that *impossible* concept for good. It's not going to be easy sailing, but do as I say and you will keep on sailing—you will keep it going."

Within a month the young couple had taken in enough money to keep their heads above water. And gradually they began making a little profit. They survived the depression, and all because they heeded the wise counsel of a friend and took a new look at that word "impossible."

This man Al Cliffe was one of the most intuitively wise men I have ever known. As a truth teacher he was superb in his insights and inspiration. He was a practical genius in the uses of the positive principle.

He himself learned creative and positive truth when desperately ill, so much so that he had been practically given up to die. In that moment of ultimate extremity Cliffe turned everything over to God, saying, "Thy will be done. Take me if you wish. But if it is Your will that I live, I will spend my years in teaching the amazing power of spiritual truth to overcome sickness, failure and all manner of difficulty." Always thereafter Dr. Cliffe taught a most basic truth, one that enormously benefited me personally and, similarly, thousands of others; and he expressed it in an unforgettable and felicitous phrase: "Let go and let God." This means essentially to do the best, the very best you possibly can do. Then, to quote St. Paul, ". . . having done all, to stand."[1] When you have done all you can do, what more can you do? That is the time to let it go and let God take over. With this methodology of the positive principle you need never be discouraged or defeated. Nothing is any longer impossible. On the basis of this philosophy you can always and forever keep it going.

Keep Inspiration Going by Check on Words

A sure way to keep inspiration going, strongly going, is to do a check on the words you commonly use. A word, or word combination, forms a thought symbol, so that one tends to reveal in his words the basic concept in his mind. Thoughts invariably show through in habitual word use. If you wish to know what a person is really thinking, simply listen to his usual word pattern. And to know why your own mental upbeat level declines, study carefully the downbeat words you are habitually using in daily conversation. Emerson has been quoted as saying, "Cut a vital word and it will bleed," which is to say that words are alive and have the power to create or to destroy.

Of all destructive words in common use, surely one of

[1]Ephesians 6:13.

24

the most powerful is the word *impossible*. More people may have failed by using that one word than almost any other in the English language.

"It's impossible" is the recurring depressant that puts the damper on enthusiasm and throws cold water on many a project that could otherwise be a success. It is therefore of first importance to eliminate the word *impossible* from daily speech, for such elimination will in time lessen its influence on your determinative thought processes. Then when you are motivated to reach some goal or to make something better of yourself and your situation, the concept of the impossible will no longer have sufficient force to interfere with the operation of the positive principle. You will be able to keep inspiration going with power. You will constantly be supplied and resupplied with a motivational force that will not decline but, indeed, will grow ever stronger and more vital.

Appraising yourself on the basis of past demonstrations of weakly held inspiration, you may react to these assertions with doubt, if not disbelief. The word *impossible* at once flashes up in your mind. You may complain, "It is impossible for me to maintain at steady level an upbeat, positive attitude. It is impossible for inspiration to so grab me that it can constantly govern my reactions and keep me going in the face of the difficulties that are always ganging up." If your expressions are of this type, it indicates that a frontal attack needs to be made on that word *impossible* and the failure-generating concept for which it stands.

He Tosses Out the Word "Impossible"

At the conclusion of a talk which I gave to a large sales meeting in Toronto's Massey Hall, a man came rushing backstage. His face was positively glowing. No other word could adequately describe his expression of wonderment and happiness. Obviously thrilled and excited, he insisted upon telling his story. And when I heard it, I, too, was excited. It is always a tremendous experience to meet a person to whom something significant has happened which has totally captured his personality.

"I owe everything to a story on pages 112 and 113 in your book *You Can If You Think You Can*," he declared. "It's the story about Napoleon Hill, the widely read inspirational writer, whose younger life was adversely conditioned by the word *impossible*. And this caused him to live in failure and unhappiness. He wanted to be a writer, so he bought a dictionary to become a master of words. One day it occurred to him that he must, once and for all, get rid of that hated word 'impossible.' His method was simple; with a pair of scissors he clipped it from the dictionary, crumpled it and vigorously threw it into the fire. So what do you know? I did exactly the same, and it is amazing how some really great possibles have taken the place of those miserable impossibles.

"Did you actually cut that word out of your dictionary?" I asked in amazement. My purpose was not to encourage mutilation of dictionaries but, rather, to motivate impossibility-type thinkers to cut the concept from their mentalities.

"I needed something dramatic," he replied. "Always before, I would get fired up to some new goal or get going on some exciting project. Then the fear that I could not do it would creep in to chill my enthusiasm. and the concept 'impossible' would take over. Result—I was washed up, licked, defeated. But I've tossed out that word *impossible* for good. And now when I get inspired I've got what it takes to keep it going. I've bought the positive principle and I don't mean maybe."

I was not surprised to discover that the change in this

26

man's attitudes had a spiritual source, for he took from his pocket a copy of our regular monthly publication *Creative Help for Daily Living*. In this periodical are published my talks given every Sunday at Marble Collegiate Church on Fifth Avenue in New York City and mailed to hundreds of thousands of recipients in every state and 110 foreign countries.[2] This particular issue contained a message entitled "Take a New Look at the Impossible," and he had underscored a passage which read:

> What are the most pathetic, the saddest, most sinister words in the English language? John Greenleaf Whittier's answer:
>
> > For of all sad words of tongue or pen,
> > The saddest are these:
> > It might have been!

That does indeed rate high as a sad expression. And there may be other nominations as well. But actually the word "impossible" is perhaps the most pathetic word in the English language. And it is unfortunate that this word is engraved so vividly on the consciousness of hundreds of thousands of people, reminding them constantly that they cannot do it; they can't make it; they haven't got it. And so they are defeated by blown-up, impressive, so-called impossibles.

What shall one do about those big obstacles, those huge, dreamed-up impossibles? When did you last speak the word "impossible"? Are you going to acquiesce supinely with the false notion that your situation is impossible? Are you about to let it throw you? It is a

[2] If you would like to receive *Creative Help for Daily Living* regularly, write me c/o the Foundation for Christian Living, Pawling, N.Y. 12564, U.S.A. There is no charge for this publication, which is supported entirely by voluntary contributions.

very important decision; what to do about those so-called impossibles that have harassed and defeated you for so long.

Take a new look at your present "impossible." Consider positive ways to handle it. Start by studying the New Testament, which is packed full of ideas about dealing with the impossible, and which should be thought of as a textbook of the positive principle. It presents the workable formula for turning the "impossible" into great possibles. For example, think about this terrific truth: "The things which are impossible with men are possible with God."[3] That is to say, if a person gets going with faith in God, with belief in tapping Divine power, then his situation becomes at once no longer impossible, because "the things which are impossible with men are possible with God." It is just that simple.

And consider that other amazing statement: "If ye have faith as a grain of mustard seed . . ."[4] Did you ever see a grain of mustard seed? Put it in your hand and the wind will blow it away. It is very small. So even if you have only a little faith like a grain of mustard seed, if it is real, "nothing"—and we mean *nothing*—"shall be impossible unto you."

There are many negative thinkers today who will eagerly tell you dogmatically that this sort of thing just isn't so, and they marshal argument after argument to bolster the negative, since it is their nature always to decry the positives. And why? Perhaps because they do not want success or victory. Strange, but some people are happier being defeated; they have the will to fail—a sick mental attitude. Nor do they want anyone else to succeed. Could be they actually want things to go badly so that they may further complain and criticize, or be-

[3]Luke 18:27.
[4]Matthew 17:20.

cause it equates wtih their own failure pattern. But an intelligent, straight thinker will go for a big structured concept of spiritual truth when convinced that it has worked miracles in the experience of many previously defeated persons.

So take a new look at that impossible. Rise above it mentally so that you attain the position of looking down on your problem. All generals who have won important victories have maneuvered to higher ground. Any person wanting to overcome a problem must get above the problem in his thought processes. Then it does not appear nearly so formidable; and he has greater confidence in his ability to deal with it.

I have spent many years endeavoring to persuade people of the fact that they possess a built-in inner power to withstand and overcome all the blows that circumstances can bring to bear upon them. There are thousands, perhaps hundreds of thousands, who have heard this message and responded exultantly to the power of positive thinking. Inspired and filled with dynamic spirit, life for them has taken on new and joyous meaning. They have discovered the power—the wonderful power to keep motivation going.

When, as is common in the experience of every person on earth, challenges to inspiration come, positive confidence may undergo acute stress. Sickness, sorrow, frustration, financial problems, personal hardship and many other vicissitudes draw so heavily upon personal resources that the erosion, perhaps even collapse, of built-up inspiration can and often does result.

Letters by the hundreds come from readers, saying, in effect: "I have followed your positive teaching and it gave me courage, strength and real happiness. But now this terrible thing has occurred and my faith is shaken. How can I keep from giving up? How can I keep the positive principle going?"

Down to $1.76

Take, for example, the woman, a regular reader of our publication, *Creative Help for Daily Living*, who in a period of severe recession wrote me of her struggle to maintain a positive faith. She told me she had that day exactly $1.76 in the bank. In addition, the firm employing her husband had been able to give only a moderate cost-of-living increase to employees, and with inflationary prices it was very hard to keep going. "But," she said, "I hold the sure faith that God will take care of us if we keep our spiritual and mental attitudes at high level. My husband and I have decided not to panic, to think positively and to keep our faith going strong."

Some weeks later, in answer to our letter of reassurance and caring concern, she wrote again describing the most "surprising occurrences" in which a new source of additional income came about, a modest amount but helpful. By refusing to panic, by keeping her courage up, her faith strong, her thinking sound, the impossibility concept which might have frustrated such a good outcome had no negative influence in this human and rather common domestic situation.

Physical Trouble Couldn't Build Up Impossibles

How can you keep your upbeat mind level going on a sustained basis when a physical problem develops? By what method may inspirational attitudes be maintained when some devastating blow strikes and undermines your health, your strength and your well-being? These are questions asked by uncounted thousands every day, everywhere.

Take, for example, the experience of Chet Craig, a

friend of mine, a dedicated positive thinker, who was always working at building up his body, sometimes jogging as much as a hundred miles a month. Suddenly one day a severe pain, and next, an operation for cancer of the prostate. But he kept his spirit going, even so. "I have to work with my mind so that diseased thoughts do not grow, as diseased tissue has grown in my body. I'm keeping on top of it all," he declared positively. "I'm going to come out on top." And latest reports indicate that he is indeed doing just that. The positive principle sustains him.

Again, there was a man whom I always think of as one of the inspiring persons I have encountered over the years. I was on a program to speak to a couple of thousand salespeople in Omaha, and before coming on for my talk this famous industrial psychologist preceded me. He could not stand, being paralyzed in both legs. But for sure he was not paralyzed in his head, for he made a brilliant speech, sitting in his wheelchair. As the members of the large audience listened, it was only for a moment that anyone was interested out of pity. He was caustic, abrasive, persuasive, kindly, humorous. He had everything a man needs to be an effective communicator, a powerful public speaker.

Later when I commented on his magnificent performance, expressing admiration by saying that I found it rough going to hold a crowd while standing on two feet, he replied, "Brains aren't in the legs. They are in the head. My legs are paralyzed, but so far my head is in working order. I've found that I can live my life minus workable legs because I still possess a workable brain."

Obviously, both of these men had an inner inspiration, a built-in motivation that enabled them to keep going against physical adversity. Both of them scoffed at the word "impossible." "What do you mean, impossible?" they each told me. "Forget it. I think in terms of the possible." They had taken a look at that word "impossible" and obviously were not impressed.

He Drew Upon a Deep Source in Tragedy

But there are greater stresses than financial stringency or even problems of health, notably those tragic events that now and then occur in human experience, such as the sudden and violent death of dear ones. Such times try the spirit to the utmost breaking point to such an extent that the word "impossible" exerts a menacing power that requires deep and extraordinary resources to meet and deal effectively with it.

My wife, Ruth, recently spoke to a conference of eleven thousand Baptist pastors in the huge auditorium at Miami Beach at a meeting presided over by my friend, Dr. James L. Pleitz, of Pensacola. The only woman to address this large and important gathering, Ruth showed me the program of the event and I noted that it contained the words of the songs to be used in the convention. One of them was by the late Luther H. Bridgers, another friend of many years and a masterful leader of gospel singing; it was called "He Keeps Me Singing."

This reminded me of the time Luther Bridgers invited me to his home for breakfast, and we had a happy time of friendship together with his family. I discovered that this was his second family group. He told of an earlier tragedy when as a young pastor he went to another city to participate in a series of meetings. One night late he was awakened by the telephone. Hesitantly over the wire came the voice of a friend telling him the almost incredible news that fire had swept through his home while his wife and two children were sleeping.

Every effort was made to save them, but the flames were too far advanced and the three members of his family perished in the holocaust that ravaged the house.

Stunned, Luther dropped the receiver and sat in agony of spirit. It couldn't be true! It just could not be true! Anguished, he paced the floor. Then he bolted from the room and out of the hotel into the early-morning emptiness of the streets. For a long time he walked up and down, desperately fighting for self-control.

Then in his search for peace he came to the river which flowed wide and deep through the town. He regarded it with fascination. In its cool depths lay forgetfulness. It would require only a moment of struggle for his spirit to leave his body and be reunited with his wife and little children. Life was so utterly impossible now. Impossible! Impossible! The word hammered at his brain. It was impossible to go on. He must die now in that swift-moving stream.

But deep within his mind was a long-established faith and a love of God as his Father. The struggle was intense. He dropped finally to his knees, and the tears that had not yet come from dry eyes now poured out in a flood. Along with the tears was a prayer in depth asking for understanding and strength to handle this tragedy with the power vouchsafed to a true believer. The struggle was long and hard, but he found his way back. Later he married again and raised a second family in whose home I had breakfasted that morning.

Completing his story, Luther sat at the piano and played movingly and with deep meaning some of the famous compositions of the great composers. Then finally he went into one of his own well-known songs. I shall never cease to be moved in memory of this strong man singing words known to thousands:

> Jesus, Jesus, Jesus,
> Sweetest name I know,
> Fills my ev'ry longing,
> Keeps me singing as I go.[5]

Golden sunlight streamed into the room, lighting up the face of the singer. As he sang, a canary in a cage above the piano also began to sing. And I am sure it was not in imagination that man and bird seemed in perfect attunement as together they poured forth praise to the Lord who gives victory of such magnitude to human beings. And who knows? Perhaps to birds also. At any rate, the sum and substance of the matter is that even in such ultimate tragedy as he experienced, Luther Bridgers knew how to keep the positive principle going. Faith of this caliber never recognizes the word or concept "impossible."

One of the chief lessons or truths to be learned by thoughtful people is that the so-called impossible is indeed possible to those who have the will, the courage and the faith. Built into the fabric of human existence is the fact that whatever is proper for man to attain or accomplish is possible for him to achieve. Marcus Aurelius phrased it potently: "Do not think that what is hard for thee to master is impossible for man; but if a thing is possible and proper to man, deem it attainable by thee."[6] Those things that an individual can conceive in the mind may be achieved by the use of the mind. Samuel Johnson declared that "few things are impossible to diligence and skill."[7] Berton Braley summed it up in a swinging sort of verse:

> Got any river they say isn't crossable?
> Got any mountains that can't be cut through?

---

[5]"He Keeps Me Singing" by Luther B. Bridgers
[6]*Meditations VI*, 19.
[7]*Rasselas*, Chap. 1.

> We specialize in the wholly impossible
> Doing things "nobody ever could do."[8]

So take a new look, shall we say a masterful new look, at that word "impossible." Rebuild your motivation. Become a specialist in doing the wholly impossible. And keep the positive principle going.

Now a sum-up of the basic points made in this chapter:

1. Cut the "im" out of impossible, leaving that dynamic word standing out free and clear—*possible*.
2. Do all you can about a tough situation; then let go and let God.
3. Never use the word "impossible" seriously again. Toss it into the verbal wastebasket.
4. Practice the positive principle—the principle of the possible. "If ye have faith . . . nothing shall be impossible unto you."[9]
5. Store up a body of indomitable faith sufficient to draw upon in crisis to sustain you.
6. Whatever is proper to a human being may be considered to be attainable by him.
7. Become a specialist in doing the "wholly impossible," the things that "can't" be done.
8. A new, straight look at that word "impossible" will make it possible always to keep your motivation going.

---

[8]"At Your Service; The Panama Gang."
[9]Matthew 17:20.

THIRD
WAY TO KEEP
THE POSITIVE
PRINCIPLE GOING

Hold the Thought
That Nothing Can
Get You Down

It is surprising how many things get so many people down. And usually they are not the big things, the great tragedies, but rather the smaller, pesky frustrations and irritations. These seem to be the real depressants of spirit, for human beings possess deep within themselves an amazing power to meet the big issues.

For example, consider the case of Major H. P. S. Ahluwalia, of India, who climbed Everest, the highest mountain on earth. With incredible exhilaration he stood finally on that great and colossal peak. But now Major Ahluwalia cannot even climb from the garden to his door. He was shot in the neck by a Pakistani sniper in Kashmir, ironically after the cease-fire between the two countries was declared and hostilities had ceased. His only locomotion now is by wheelchair—this man whose powerful legs and sturdy heart carried him to the summit of the world's highest eminence.

But did this super tragedy get him down? Well, hardly. He was able to overcome a profound depression and, to use his own felicitous phrase, he "climbed the Everest within." And, explained the major, to stand on the peak of himself after struggling wtih his own spirit was every bit as exhilarating as the thrill of standing on the summit of the vast mountain. He dramatically demonstrated that nothing can really get a person down provided he has learned the skill, the ability, the power to keep it going.

Perhaps few readers of this book will ever face a challenge to the spirit even remotely comparable to that of Major Ahluwalia. But nearly everyone has to deal with daily irritations, monotony and those annoyances that take a toll of inspiration and motivational vitality. To keep it going in the presence of cumulative frustrations certainly isn't easy.

Common frustration sometimes takes quite uncommon forms and expressions. As, for example, the housewife who got completely fed up with the constant and unending annoyances to which she felt desperately subjected. In a moment of feeling quite unable to cope with them anymore, she simply set fire to the house and walked away without looking back! I read this little human tempest and furor story in a newspaper somewhere.

Then there was the case of the quiet and submissive husband who had meekly and supinely given in for years to his irritable and nagging wife. But the pent-up frustration within the husbandly breast finally broke through. Still true to his uncombative nature, the harassed man left home one morning without a word and was gone for twenty-five years. Then he returned home and the wife reported that he was much easier to get along with than before. As to his own reactions, no report was forthcoming, but this time he stayed. This story I also read in some forgotten daily sheet in which were recounted the foibles of human nature.

In another book[1] I told about a curious incident of frustration and irritation and their power to get one down. It concerned the businessman who had turned

[1] *Positive Thinking for a Time Like This.*

home and office into a hell because of his temper tantrums, his acute lack of self-control. He was, as his wife and office associates described it, always "hitting the ceiling." It appears that his asperity and annoyance were so sharp and continuous that the ceiling was his usual habitat.

The Worm Turns

But one day "the worm turned." He had been storming about the house violently declaiming that he could no longer take it and that everything was getting him down. The tirade was laced with salty and sulfurous words.

About the worm turning. His wife had endured all that she could take. With eyes blazing, she shoved him into a chair and stood before him in unabashed fury. "Now you just listen to me and don't you say a word. I've let you shout and fume and swear until I am completely sick of it. It's my turn, and you sit there and listen until I get through with you." Whereupon she proceeded to lay him out with a sharp, clear picture of the mean, irritable, self-centered person he had become.

It wasn't only things that were getting him down, she declared. He was getting himself down, victimized by his raw, nervous state in which frustration compounded irritation until she and everyone else found it impossible to deal with him or, indeed, to endure him.

While his wife belabored him, suddenly she seemed to fade from his sight. He was no longer aware of her, or of the room in which this dialogue was proceeding. Instead, he seemed to be standing on a strange riverbank along which flowed a slow-moving current, and there in midstream was a dark, even repulsive object bobbing sluggishly. Suddenly he was sharply aware that he was seeing within himself the stream of his own selfhood. And that dark and ugly thing floating sluggishly he now realized was the error and evil in his nature. This was the source of his uptight tension that would finally destroy him unless quickly contained. This he saw clearly and without doubt.

The vision passed gradually to reveal the highly exercised wife still vehemently excoriating her husband, but now she regarded him quizzically. Startled, she fell into bewildered silence. "I see myself clearly," he said, rather awed. "Never before have I had a sharp insight into my own self. I now know that I must break up that inner failure center. Because out of it seem to rise the irritants that goad me into unreasonableness."

This story represents a curious demonstration of the cumulative effect of frustrations built up and up. The man involved, due to his acute and extraordinary revelation of self-knowledge, recovered his shattered sense of balance. He operated thereafter on an organized motivational basis. His personality normalized. A new control over frustrating and irritating factors enabled him to hold firmly to the conviction that nothing could get him down. He relearned the ability to keep the positive principle going effectively by authoritatively containing hitherto uncontrolled emotional reaction.

Frustrated Canadian Finds Answer

The struggle with the irritations and exasperations which plague so many and the possible solutions to overcoming them were illustrated in the experience of a man from Canada. "I just could not go on with it," he declared. He therefore left home without any explanation to anyone and took off in his car for New York. He had only one objective in mind—to sign on as a deckhand on a slow freighter bound for some distant port, he did not care where. Anywhere that would put distance between his home and himself was all that he wanted.

He arrived in New York on a Saturday to find that port activities were shut down until Monday. He wandered aimlessly about the city, trying for forgetfulness in movie houses, but they all left him cold. On Sunday morning, still aimlessly walking, he found himself on Fifth Avenue. There he was surprised to see crowds of people lined up to go into a church. Never before having seen a crowd queued up for church, he joined the line more in curiosity than in a desire to go to church, and he was lucky to get the last seat in the last row.

Five years later this man wrote me to tell of his experience that Sunday morning. Looking about him, he noticed that the people were both black and white, indeed persons of various races and of all ages, lots of young people, the congregation seeming to consist of perhaps more than 50 percent men. Everyone appeared friendly, and a strange feeling that he finally decided to call love plus excitement seemed to pervade the atmosphere.

As he listened to the outstanding choir and the reading of verses from the Scriptures and the prayers, and hesitantly participated in the enthusiastic singing of old familiar hymns, he began to have a warm feeling of belonging. Memories of "the good days of my youth stirred within my mind. A profound sense of peace filled my heart. Tears came to my eyes as I sat within your great stone refuge."

The service came to a close and the big congregation began to leave the church. Everybody seemed uplifted, renewed, happy. Then the lady he had been sitting beside offered her hand in greeting and all she said was, "God loves you." That was enough. It broke him up. Out on the avenue he walked for blocks, and it was like walking on air. He knew that he could cope—cope with anything. He now believed with deepening certainty that he could rise above all frustration. This new motivational inspiration that he strongly felt was surely the real thing, and he had no doubt that it would keep him going and that he could keep it going. Which is precisely what he did. He immediately drove home to Canada and was still going strong when five years later he wrote of the experience which taught him the dynamic truth that nothing need keep you down.

Life Can Be Tough, Very Tough

That life on earth has a powerful crushing quality can hardly be denied. Circumstances relating to health, job, money, hostility, misunderstanding, and numerous other adversaries of well-being are constantly making it difficult, if not downright painful, for multitudes of people every day. Little wonder that the psychoanalyst Freud is reported to have said, "The chief duty of a human being is to endure life." And life can indeed be tough, very tough.

In a profound sense it is true that a chief, if not *the* chief, duty of any of us is simply to endure what life brings. There are certain inevitables with which one must live. Learning to live with some painful disability, because no release formula has been found, is in itself an achievement.

My father was a very happy and creative man. In middle life he developed a painful arthritic condition which bothered him no end. "Almost got me down," he admitted. "But I outsmarted it. I finally learned that it could not be cured, only palliated. So I accepted that fact and learned to live with it." He never talked much about it in later years and lived to celebrate his eighty-fifth birthday. One thing is sure: It never got him down—not at all. He even declared that it seemed less painful when he accepted it as an inevitable with which he must get along. He applied the positive principle to that physical problem.

With due respect to the "endure it" principle, which often makes the difficulties of human existence pretty grim, there is another attitude that is upbeat, called the "master it" principle. Basically, nothing can get you down if you use that quality deep within your human nature that resists defeat, the upthrusting force designed to meet and overcome any crushing element in your experience. One potent sentence may describe it: "This is the victory that overcometh the world, even our faith."[2] Faith is the most powerful of all forces operating in humanity, and when you have it in depth, nothing can get you down. *Nothing.* This is the positive principle, and it is full of healing power.

Dwarf Becomes a Giant

If you consider yourself weak and inadequate and lacking in power to stand up to life's challenges and rigorous difficulties, you are taking an erroneous view of yourself. You simply are not so inadequate and lacking in strength as you assume yourself to be. Indeed, such assumption is dangerous, for it tends to create the fact. You are likely to build a case against yourself if you continue such thoughts. This process of self-limitation and self-depreciation is seldom expressed outwardly where you put on a front. But it does work in consciousness. And upon emphasis and re-emphasis, it can and often does pass, by mental osmosis, into the unconscious, where it may become determinative.

This results in an individual's attempts to put down

[2] I John 5:4.

the giant that the Creator has placed at the center of every personality. For there is a giant in every person, and nothing can get this giant down unless that giant is kept down by himself.

Ernie Belz had a frozen personality when he first arrived in America from Europe. He was so abnormally short of stature (only a little over four feet) that he had developed a deep-seated inferiority feeling. A thirty-year-old Swiss, who had come to the United States hoping to find himself, Ernie discovered it hard going at first.

His broken English usually brought a smile, and his minuscule size was always a handicap. Mounting a bus, he could not negotiate the step but had to swing himself up. When he went into a store for clothing, he was referred to the boys' department.

One day Ernie Belz was lunching alone in a restaurant when a young man from Marble Collegiate Church invited him to our Young Adults Group. He accepted and received friendship and understanding instead of the curious looks to which he was accustomed. But the thawing of a frozen personality does not happen in a day—or a month.

A big turning point came one night at a Young Adults meeting when a member spoke convincingly on the theme "God Has a Plan for My Life." Ernie had some questions about this idea. "Do I understand that you really believe God has a plan for my life, a little fellow like me?" Ernie asked doubtfully.

"Sure—God has a plan for every one of us, and this means you, too, Ernie. The problem is you must be willing to do whatever He wants you to do."

In other meetings with these spiritually alive and with-it young people, he was shown that size or color or handicap had nothing to do with how much or how effective one could become.

As a result of this encouragement, Ernie began to think more creatively. He learned the positive principle. He stopped trying to lose himself in crowds and began to take an interest in others as individuals. He volunteered for church work projects. He also developed the art of discovering other persons' interests and bringing out the best in each individual's personality.

Good things began happening to Ernie Belz. One was that he escaped from his shell of inferiority and became a released individual. Several years later he secured an administrative job with an educational institution in Africa.

Ernie must have grown and grown big in this job, for an executive under whom he worked wrote: "How much better this world would be if we had more people like Ernie Belz. He may be small in physical stature, but actually he is a giant when it comes to helping other people find themselves."

All the time there was an undetected giant in Ernie Belz. And that giant finally emerged to disclose a man with dynamic motivation and power to keep the positive principle going and influence everyone he met. By the same line of factual reasoning, there is a giant in you, too. When that giant takes charge, nothing can get you down, ever.

You Can Do Incredible Things

When that inner giant is alive and vital, you are no longer hampered by negative and inferiority thoughts. When you are packed full of faith in God and in yourself, you can do just about anything you firmly and authoritatively decide to do. When you wholeheartedly

45

adopt a "with all your heart" attitude and go all out with the positive principle, you can do incredible things. Strange, the tendency of some skeptics to disparage such an assertion as "You can do just about anything you decide to do." Actually, I am minded to drop those two qualifying words, "just about," especially when I recall the amazing story of Legson Kayira, a teen-ager living in a tiny African village who walked a distance of 2,500 miles across the continent and then made his way to the American West Coast—but let him tell the story in his own words. "Barefoot to America," he calls his incredible tale.[3]

> My mother did not know where America was. I said to her, "Mother, I want to go to America to go to college. Will you give me your permission?"
>
> "Very well," she said. "You may go. When will you leave?"
>
> I did not want to give her time to discover how far away America was, for fear that she would change her mind. "Tomorrow," I said.
>
> "I will prepare some maize for you to eat along the way," she said.
>
> Next day I left my home in northern Nyasaland, East Africa. I had only the clothes I wore, a khaki shirt and shorts. I carried the two treasures I owned: a Bible and a copy of *Pilgrim's Progress*. I carried, too, the maize my mother had given me, wrapped in banana leaves.
>
> My goal was a continent and an ocean away, but I did not doubt that I would reach it. I had no idea how old I was. Such things mean little in a land where time is always the same. I suppose I was 16 or 18. My father died when I was very young. My mother listened to the words of the missionaries, with the result that our family became Christian.
>
> From the missionaries I learned I was not the victim of circumstances but the master of them. I learned

[3]*Guideposts* magazine.

that I had an obligation to use whatever talents I had to make life better for others. And to do that I would need education. I learned about America. I read the life of Abraham Lincoln and grew to love this man who suffered so much to help the enslaved in his country. I read, too, the autobiography of Booker T. Washington, himself born in slavery in America, and who had risen in dignity and honor to become a benefactor of his people and his country.

I gradually realized that in America I could receive the training and opportunities to prepare myself to emulate these men in my own land, to be, like them, a leader, perhaps even the president of my country.

My intention was to make my way to Cairo, where I hoped to get passage on a ship to America. Cairo was over 3,000 miles away, a distance I could not comprehend, and I foolishly thought I could walk it in four or five days. But in four or five days I was about 25 miles from home, my food was gone, I had no money, and I did not know what to do, except that I must keep going.

I developed a pattern of travel that became my life for more than a year. Villages were usually five or six miles apart, on forest paths. I would arrive at one in the afternoon and ask if I could work to earn food, water and a place to sleep. When this was possible, I would spend the night there. then move on to the next village in the morning. I was actually defenseless against the forest animals I dreaded. but although I heard them at night none of them approached me. Malaria mosquitoes, however, were constant companions, and I often was sick.

By the end of a year I had walked 1,000 miles and had arrived in Uganda, where a family took me in and I found a job making bricks. I remained there six months and sent most of my earnings to my mother.

In Kampala, I unexpectedly came upon a directory of American colleges. Opening it at random, I saw the name of Skagit Valley College, Mount Vernon, Washington. I had heard that American colleges sometimes give scholarships to deserving young people, so I wrote and applied for one. I realized that I might be refused but was not discouraged: I would write to one school after another in the directory until I found one that would help me.

Three weeks later I was granted a scholarship and assured that the school would help me find a job. Overjoyed, I went to the United States authorities, only to be told that this was not enough. I would need a passport and the round-trip fare in order to obtain a visa.

I wrote to my government for a passport but it was refused because I could not tell them when I was born. I then wrote to the missionaries who had taught me in my childhood, and through their efforts was granted a passport. But I still could not get the visa because I did not have the fare.

Still determined, I resumed my journey. So strong was my faith that I used my last money to buy my first pair of shoes: I knew I could not walk into college in my bare feet. I carried the shoes to save them.

Across Uganda and into the Sudan I walked. The villages were farther apart and the people were less friendly. Sometimes I had to walk 20 or 30 miles in a day to find a place to sleep or to work to earn some food. At last I reached Khartoum, where I learned that there was a United States consulate.

Once again I heard about the U.S. entrance requirements, but this time the Consul was interested enough to write the college about my plight. Back came a cable.

The students, hearing about me and my problems, had raised the fare of $1,700 through benefit parties. I was thrilled and deeply grateful; overjoyed that I had judged Americans correctly for their friendship and brotherhood.

News that I had walked for over two years and 2,500 miles circulated in Khartoum. The Communists came to me and offered to send me to school in Yugoslavia, all expenses paid, including travel, and a subsistence during my studies. "I am a Christian," I told them, "and I could not be educated into the kind of man I want to be in your godless schools." They warned me that, as a black boy, I would have racial difficulties in the United States, but I had read enough to feel this was a diminishing factor.

After many, many months, carrying my two books and wearing my first suit, I arrived at Skagit Valley College. In my speech of gratitude to the student body I disclosed my desire to become prime minister or president of my country, and I noticed some smiles. I wondered if I had said something naïve. I do not think so.

When God has put an impossible dream in your heart, He means to help you fulfill it. I believed this to be true when, as an African bush boy, I felt compelled to become an American college graduate. And my dream of becoming president of Nyasaland can also become true.

Story Update

To update the story, Mr. Kayira is still walking up and forward with his inner giant, and walking strong. He never fails to live by the positive principle. He became professor of political science at Cambridge University in England. He has authored a novel, *The Looming Shadow*, and a nonfiction book based on African life.

What do you mean, you can't do anything? What do you mean, things can get you down? Not when you have the urge, the impulse, the motivation, to keep it going, to everlastingly keep it going. Hold that thought and hold it strong and sturdy—that nothing can ever get you down. If you think you are down, tell you what . . . do not stay down. Get right up; shake off defeat. Reactivate the giant within you and get going—and keep it going. Live always by the amazing positive principle. That is the realistic and proven philosophy that succeeds and keeps on succeeding.

How to Hit It Again and Keep Going

But suppose you have already been knocked down before you started reading this book and have accepted the negative thought that you are down and guess you are down for good. What then? Change your attitude, really change it. Simply start affirming: "I do not mean to stay down. What an advantage to have hit bottom. I will never minimize the value of the bottom, for it is a very advantageous place to be. The bottom is as far down as I can go. The only direction from here is up. And up I am going."

So, then, start looking up. Start thinking up. Begin acting in an up manner. And keep going in an up direction, no matter how steep or how long the climb. If you keep thinking positively, affirming positively, acting positively, always practicing the positive principle, the way will clear and you will reach that greatly-to-be-desired top away up there. With this spirit, that top is not all that far off, and this time you will stay there, having learned how always to keep it going.

Executive, Fifty-two, Loses Job, But—

A friend, at fifty-two, was operating vice-president of an apparently strong manufacturing company. He was an engineer by profession, with outstanding managerial ability. Then two adverse conditions arose: a recessionary period and some innovative inventions by a competitor which rendered his firm's line practically obsolete. The company failed at a time when jobs were scarce, especially for men over fifty. Finally the unhappy situation got to where he would have to take whatever kind of employment he could get. He wasn't proud; he simply wanted to work. Indeed, he had to work. He knocked on lots of doors. "Sorry, but nothing now. Leave your name." So it went, day after day.

Finally one employment manager, looking over his résumé, hesitantly said, "You have good engineering experience. We don't need anyone right now, but there may be a vacancy later in a small, and I'm sure for you uninteresting, job with us. You see, the trouble is that you are overqualified."

"Overqualified, nothing. As an engineer, I can handle a broom. I'll prove to be the best sweeper-outer you ever had in this place." He was actually hired as a janitor's assistant, a clean-up man.

But to his menial job he applied his organizational know-how, so much so that he finished every job in record time and was back for more assignments. Each minor job was done not only quickly but in an innovative way that saved time and effort.

Later he became divisional manager of that organization and last I heard he was headed for that place that may be called the antithesis of the bottom—namely, the top.

You do not need to let anything get you down, but if you are down you certainly need not let anything keep you down.

Art Fleming's Method for Keeping It Going

I like the way Art Fleming, famous host-star of the long-time television show *Jeopardy*, handled the matter of not letting anything get him down. Art knows how to keep it going. He lives by the positive principle.

You see, Art is a deacon in my church and knows how to handle a tough matter spiritually. And that, of course, is the only sound basis on which to deal with anything of importance.

Here is how Art reacted to the news that his long-running and popular quiz program was being dropped, according to Steve Tinney of the *National Enquirer*:

> "I'm not the least bit upset about it," the famous emcee said. "In fact, I can't wait to see what God has in store for me. It may sound strange, but I really believe every time one door closes, another, even better one, opens. My life," he continued, "has always been in the hands of God and knowing that gives me a positive mental attitude. I can accept whatever He has in store for me and whatever it is, it'll be better than *Jeopardy*—I just know it.
>
> "I don't claim to be holier than thou," Fleming said. "But the way I see it, if God is for me, who can be against me? My inspiration and guidance come from my everyday conversations with God. I thank Him for each and every day—regardless of what happens."

Fleming then told how, saddened by the death of his father some years ago, he was so hard hit that he took off for the wilds of Canada where there was no telephone, no contact with the outside world. While there, a prominent manufacturer tried to reach him with an attractive offer to promote his merchandise on television, but, unable to reach him, signed someone else to the lucrative contract. Art admits to disappointment when he returned, but then he got the *Jeopardy* offer, which he held for eleven years, and which he would have missed had he been around to accept the first offer.

"God watches out for all of us," Fleming concluded. "When things go wrong, He's strengthening you for even better things to come."

So firmly hold the thought that nothing can get you down and keep the positive principle going—always keep it going.

Remember:

1. Don't be concerned about your ability to handle the big disasters; shore yourself up against the little irritations and frustrations.
2. Always remember when frustrated that it isn't all that bad—and that God loves you.
3. Know for sure that there is a giant within you. And then release the giant YOU.
4. Remember and never doubt it—with God's help you can do incredible things.
5. Never think down—always think up.
6. Put problems into God's hands and leave them there. He will take care of you and bring things out right.

FOURTH
WAY TO KEEP
THE POSITIVE
PRINCIPLE GOING

Get Turned On With
Self-Repeating Enthusiasm

It happened on a Fifth Avenue bus in New York. A friend of mine came aboard and sank with a sigh into the seat alongside of me. "Hello, Mr. Positive Thinking, you're just the guy I need. Fancy meeting you here."

"How come?" I asked. "Please elucidate." We were old friends and banter was the usual procedure.

"Boy, am I out of enthusiasm! And listen, don't start giving me any of that positive stuff. Look, I've had about a dozen bad breaks and everything has gone wrong lately. Not a thing has gone right, not a thing."

So saying, he started reeling off the dozen bad breaks, but I noticed that after about four of them he slowed down and with an effort could not get beyond six. "You sure are a poor counter, or else you have an over-developed imagination," I remarked. "You said you had a dozen bad breaks and yet you can only come up with six. Why the exaggeration?"

"Well," he hesitated, "it seems like a dozen, even more like a hundred. Anyway, all that old enthusiasm you got me started with the last time I heard you make a speech has gone down the drain."

"Pretty thin enthusiasm, if you ask me, to go down the drain that fast just because you've had a couple of bad breaks which anybody with any stuff on the ball could handle without all this dramatization. In my opinion

55

you're overplaying it. Anyway, what you need is not a vacuous enthusiasm that runs out of you at the first sign of a little difficulty. Here's my suggestion: get turned on—really turned on—with a self-repeating enthusiasm. And to do that, think, pray and act with enthusiasm until it takes over in you."

"Okay, okay, thanks for the sermon. I'll try it," he said as we left the bus and separated at the corner of Fifty-seventh Street. I'm glad to report that he made the grade all right. And he did so by a buildup of enthusiasm that lent enhanced power to all of his activities. In fact, he was doing all right when I rode the bus with him, but he was just talking wrong. That in itself is dangerous, for wrong talking can lead to wrong thinking, and then you can get into real trouble.

Funny thing, how some people get turned on with a self-repeating enthusiasm and remain turned on regardless of a lot of things that might turn it off . . . and as a matter of fact do turn it off in a great many desultory-reacting individuals.

But there are others, more than might be imagined, who have learned the skill of an enthusiasm that is self-renewing. They really know how to keep the positive principle going. Like the lady of ninety years whom I saw in Ontario. I was about to describe her as an old lady, but since she really isn't that except chronologically, I will bypass the word "old" as inexact in her case. At any rate, she is a shining example of the positive principle in action.

Her Source of Self-Repeating Enthusiasm

The woman was in a wheelchair. One leg had been amputated, but enthusiastically she described how, though she lived alone, she did all her own housework from that wheelchair, even to running a vacuum cleaner, cooking meals and making the bed. "Must be tough going," I commented.

"Not if you know the tricks, and I know 'em. Have to. Nobody else around, and I can't get help. Couldn't pay for a girl if one could be found. But don't worry; I'm not complaining, I enjoy it," she concluded vigorously.

"How long have you been without that leg?" I asked.

"Oh, about five years. Sure could use it. And if I had it I'd be on the go a lot more."

"You get out even with that wheelchair?"

"Of course. Do you expect me to stay cooped up in this house all the time?"

"This dynamic ninety-year-old runs the rest of us ragged," said her twenty-seven-year-old granddaughter, who added, "I drop in every other day just to get a new shot of enthusiasm from Grandma. Mine runs down so easily."

"But don't you ever get discouraged?" I asked this elderly female ball of fire.

"Discouraged? Of course I do."

"And what do you do when you get discouraged?" I prodded.

"Why, I just get over it. What else is there to do?"

"Okay. That's the best answer I ever heard. And what about all this enthusiasm you exhibit—how did you come by it? And, more important still, how do you keep it going, what with one leg and this wheelchair and being ninety and all that?"

"Listen, son," she said, pointing a finger at me (and believe me, I went for that "son" business), "here's the way it is. I read the Bible and I believe what it says, and one thing I keep repeating is this: 'I am come that they might have life, and that they might have it more abundantly.'[1] And do you know something? The Bible

[1]John 10:10.

doesn't qualify that promise by saying except if you are in a wheelchair minus a leg and if you are ninety years old, or what. It just promises abundant life—period. And so I repeat this promise to myself and take abundant life and I'm happy and I have a ball."

Quite a contrast to the "old man" who told me in a half-quavering voice that he was sixty-nine and said, "Don't let anyone kid you. It's hell getting old. It's day-by-day deterioration and just plain misery. And I'd just about as soon get the whole thing over with, and fast. And," he continued, "I was full of enthusiasm once, same as you are."

"What happened to your enthusiasm?" I asked.

"I'm getting old, I tell you, and you can't be old and have enthusiasm."

Which is, of course, a dogmatic and erroneous assertion based on highly personalized, negative opinion. The fact that a ninety-year-old one-legged woman could be perpetually enthusiastic and a sixty-nine-year-old two-legged man felt otherwise does not prove his didactic assertion that one cannot be of senior status and enthusiastic simultaneously.

How One Man Got Turned On

It was a hot day in the convention hall of a Florida east coast hotel. I was the speaker at the morning session of a national convention, and could look from the platform directly out at the beach where the rolling sea was breaking in surf on the shore. That sight of the cool seawater looked good, for the air conditioning was not working too well that day. Everyone had removed his coat except me, and I was anything but comfortable. I determined to finish my talk and get out into that ocean as soon as possible.

Diving into the waves, I came up beside another

swimmer. We passed the usual greetings, then, apparently not recognizing me, the man asked, "Were you in the convention meeting this morning?"

"Yes, I was there," I replied.

"Then you heard that talk by Peale."

"Yes, I heard it."

"Well," he continued, "what did you think of it?"

I hesitated to comment upon my own speech, so I countered with, "What did you think of it?" He started to give me his opinion and, not being sure what his appraisal might be, I plunged into a convenient wave as he started talking and came up as he was finishing his comments. I said to him, "Look, my friend, I'd better level with you and tell you that I am Peale." Whereupon he plunged into a wave! I never did know his opinion. We both laughed, and after a good swim we sat on the beach and chatted for a while.

"You were talking about enthusiasm at the convention," he said, "and that is a very important quality for anyone to have. Trouble is, I get steamed up about a new project but after a while that enthusiasm starts cooling off. I just can't seem to hang in there and keep motivated. Really, I believe I could move up in our company if I didn't goof off so often. What do you suppose is wrong with a guy who has the know-how and experience but just plain runs out of gas?" This question indicated a rather common problem, and he continued, "If you've got a moment, how about giving me some practical suggestions for getting turned on and keeping it going that way?" The man seemed genuinely concerned, so I suggested the following thoughts for his consideration:

1. The secret of changing one's personality, regardless of the problem, is to think in new categories. This might mean a re-education of the thought pattern so

that enthusiasm is put into the top-priority category. To change the routine of being enthused only to have it begin to reduce, one needs to think in terms of renewal, replenishment and reinvigoration. The mind will, in time, accept the concept of undiminished supply, and this use of the positive principle will lead to perpetuity of enthusiasm.

2. Begin at once the mental practice of seeing yourself as a completely different person, an altogether new individual. This new person would be one who was never variable or mercurial but constantly the same, always vital, vigorous, excited. That which we constantly image will emerge as fact.

3. Employ creative word therapy. This means to change a personality defect by the use of corrective words. For example, a person afflicted by tension, let us say, might articulate such words as "serenity," "imperturbability," "quietness." The repetitive saying of the word tends to induce the concept for which words are symbols. So, to upgrade enthusiasm, set aside a few minutes every day to say aloud such words as "exciting," "dynamic," "marvelous," "fabulous," "terrific." I admitted that the idea might seem a bit corny, but nevertheless it is a fact that the unconscious mind will ultimately accept repetitive suggestions strongly affirmed.

4. Finally I described how helpful in maintaining my own enthusiasm at high level was the daily morning practice of a particular affirmation of enthusiasm. This one sentence has changed not a few persons from being desultory to being continually powered with enthusiasm: "This is the day that the Lord has made; I will rejoice and be glad in it."[2]

My swimming companion apparently found these suggestions of practical value, for later he reported that

[2]Psalm 118:24 (paraphrased).

he had "really put this enthusiasm formula into operation, with incredible results." What the results were he did not say, but that they proved effective was evidenced by the enthusiasm with which he reported.

Old Age and Enthusiasm

This book may be read by people who have accumulated some years, and for them, as for all of us, enthusiasm is important. I want to touch on the positive principles operational in this area (and will have more to say about this subject in Chapter 12). I like the position of Russell A. Kemp, who in his book *Live Youthfully Now*[3] says, "Time has no power to age me. We do not live by time," he points out, "but by God's creative and re-creative life force within. And that life force is not regulated by a human time system, which is an arbitrary, man-made chronology measurement. With God, 'a thousand years in thy sight are but as yesterday when it is past, and as a watch in the night.' "[4]

It is true that all our lives we are conditioned to assume that mental and physical vigor is supposed to decline after we have made, say, sixty or seventy or eighty trips around the sun on a whirling sphere called earth. I heard a man say one evening as we sat by the fireplace in his home and listened to the romantic ticking of an old Seth Thomas clock, "This clock is ticking my life away." But no instrument manufactured a hundred years or so ago can determine the quality of anyone's life. No mechanism for time measurement should cause a person one day to say, "Now I'm old; the end is near."

Old age may perhaps more properly be thought of as a state of mind in which certain mental attitudes, built by customary and traditional thinking into the conscious

[3]Published by Unity Books, Unity Village Mo. 64063.
[4]Psalm 90:4.

and unconscious mind, convince us that the life force is declining and we are therefore expected to think aged, act aged and, in fact, be aged. That fascinating description of aging in the Bible says nothing about time measurements such as minutes, days, weeks or years but refers, rather, to deteriorating mental attitudes. "When they shall be afraid of that which is high [i.e., when they shall have lost enthusiasm, or when the positive principle has sagged], and fears shall be in the way . . ."[5]

It is altogether likely that people of all ages—so-called old age as well as those of fewer or younger years—can live better, healthier, happier lives by getting turned on to self-repeating enthusiasm. The real fountain of youth is not to be discovered by a Ponce de León hunting in some magic isle, but, rather, in revitalized attitudes of mind. And certainly it is present in the dynamic thought that we can live youthfully now and always. I have never forgotten something that was said to me by former Postmaster General James A. Farley. I asked how he accounted for the seemingly slight effect the passing years had on him. His reply was classic: "I never think any old thoughts."

Live Youthfully Now

"If most of us surrender to the passing of years," says Mr. Kemp,[6] "and let them make us old, but certain others defy the passage of an even greater number of years and retain the vigor and enjoyment of life associated with youth, can it be possible that aging is really our own fault? Is the effect that passing years have on our body really an individual matter? Here is what some modern medical scientists have to say upon this point.

[5]Ecclesiastes 12:5.
[6]*Live Youthfully Now*, p. 19.

"After a conference of medical and surgical specialists at the Decourcy Clinic in Cincinnati some years ago, the following report was issued: 'Time is not toxic. All of those who develop a time-neurosis subscribe to the prevalent superstition that time is in some way a poison exerting a mysterious cumulative action . . . time has no effect on human tissues under any conditions . . . vigor does not necessarily vary inversely with the age of an adult. Belief in the effects of time by those who subscribe to such a belief is the thing that acts as a poison.'

"To put it another way, there is no scientific basis for believing, as most of us do, that the passage of years automatically causes our body to age. [And, presumably, that would go for spirit and mind as well.] 'It is ignorance of the truth about the passage of time,' the report continues, 'that causes us to cringe in fear before the accumulation of years. We need not surrender to age, if our mind is sufficiently enlightened.' "

Mr. Kemp continues by telling us that a Michigan doctor, Frederick C. Swartz, debunked the so-called infirmities of age. " 'The forgetful mind, the doddering gait, the shaky hand—these are caused by the lack of physical and mental exertion, and not by the passage of time. There are no diseases caused by the mere passage of time. Our present conception of the aging process must be shattered, and our already brainwashed oldsters made to see the nature of their ailments. Daily mental and physical exercise practiced with some degree of self-discipline should raise the life-expectancy figure ten years in one generation.'

"Dr. Swartz spoke of the fatal concept that debilities come with age, and that at sixty-five one is 'over the hill.' If accepted, this condemns one to a period of ever-narrowing horizons, until the final sparks of living are the psychoneurotic concerns with the workings of his own body."

Enthusiasm Key to Continuous Youth

One wonders if an enthusiastic young person who kept it going all his life could not restrain and slow up the aging process. A philosopher may have spoken a wise insight when he said, "The secret of genius is to carry the spirit of the child into old age." Children are by nature enthusiastic, and the effective person retains that spirit throughout his entire life. As Wordsworth has it, "Trailing clouds of glory . . . we come from God, who is our home."[7] The child remains dynamic, excited, interested, eager—until a negative time concept gets in its deadly work; and the jaded so-called sophistication of our time takes its toll; until it may be said, as the poet expressed so graphically:

> The youth, who daily farther from the east
> Must travel, still is Nature's priest,
> And by the vision splendid
> Is on his way attended;
> At length the man perceives it die away,
> And fade into the light of common day.[8]

Indeed, it could be that the saddest phenomenon in the developing life of any individual is the decay of enthusiasm. But this sad process need not take place if creative and positive thought is made a consistent practice. And, if the mind has not been disciplined to those practices that are propitious to the maintenance of enthusiasm, it is always possible to begin a program of cultivation at any time. And inevitably, with such revamping will come a powerful rebirth or rejuvenation of personality force and, who knows, perhaps of physical force as well!

[7]*Ode* "Intimations of Immortality " lines 64-65.
[8]*Ibid.* lines 71-76.

The methods for developing a self-repeating enthusiasm that will not run down may not be easy, but still they are not all that difficult, either.

A case in point is that of the professional copywriter who complained that he had gone stale in his job. Fresh ideas would no longer come. His copy ran too long and had no flow of thought or expression. It was stilted and lacked the power to communicate. "And communication is my business," he concluded glumly. The reason he gave for all this was that his enthusiasm had leaked out. Nothing seemed to motivate or activate him any longer. The bottom had dropped out of his spirit. "It's too bad," he remarked wryly, "that you cannot go to the corner drugstore and buy a bottle of enthusiasm elixir."

Medicine Not in a Bottle

"But there is a cure," I reminded him. "The medicine for it is not contained in a bottle but is a concept in your mind. And it isn't a complex procedure to get enthusiasm going again. All you need is to start acting enthusiastic and continue to so act until in time you become enthusiastic." I then called his attention to the famous principle announced by Professor William James, who was considered by some to be the father of psychological science, which he described as the "as if" principle. This means simply that by acting as you wish yourself to be, in due course you will become as you act. If you are fearful, act as if you had courage. Continue to act courageously and ultimately your fear will diminish as courage increases. If you are inclined to criticize, start acting generously, placing the best connotation on everyone and everything, and you will become less critical and more compassionate.

The principle operates similarly in the matter of increasing enthusiasm. Begin to act enthusiastically. At first the effort may appear ineffective and even phony or insincere, inasmuch as you do not feel enthusiastic. But persevere, and, surprisingly, you will become increasingly enthusiastic. It is a law of behavior described as the "as if" principle.

But I only half persuaded the glum and unenthusiastic writer, for he apparently thought the idea too simple. Being insecure, he felt that he could shore up his basic negativism only with an intellectual system of complexities. Later he attended a meeting where I was addressing a large audience of sales people on the subject "Why Positive Thinkers Get Positive Results," and made the points that successful achievement is based on these premises: 1. Cool, rational thinking, not heated emotional reaction, leads to the solution of problems. 2. Never think negatively, for the negative thinker does a very dangerous thing. He pumps out negative thoughts into the world around him and thus activates that world negatively. On the basis of the law of attraction—like attracts like—he tends to draw back to himself negative results. 3. There is value in thinking and acting enthusiastically.

As an illustration of this third point, I suggested that every man in the audience could make the next day the best in his life. The method for so doing was not to lie in bed moaning, groaning and grumbling as usual, pouring into the ears of his patient and long-suffering wife his aches, pains and negativisms. Instead, when he awoke he was to throw back the bedcovers with a gesture of masterful self-assertion and leap out of bed, exclaiming to his startled wife, "Honey, I feel wonderful."

Of course, she might very well have a heart attack and expire on the spot! But she would die happy. Then, this man was to sing in the shower, thereby washing out of mind all the old, tired, dead thoughts of yesterday while washing the body with soap and water. After this, feeling alive to the fingertips, he was to get dressed and descend to the dining room and sit down to the breakfast his wife had so thoughtfully and lovingly prepared for him. He was to take a long, respectful look at that breakfast and say, "Honey, this is by all odds the most magnificent breakfast I ever sat down to." That assuredly would inspire her so that the next day he would not need to lie about it!

Start the Day
With Enthusiastic Attitudes

Then, having put under his belt a good, man-sized breakfast, he was to go out into the crisp morning air and stand tall, reaching for the sky with the crown of his head. He was to kiss his wife good-bye with enthusiasm, and I suggested that he go so far as to pick her up and swing her around. I admitted that for some that would be quite a tussle, but it would transmit enthusiasm to her.

Then, standing in the brisk morning air, he was to say, "Honey, do you know something? I'm going to go downtown today and deal in goods and services [or sell, or write, or manage] with enthusiasm, and I'm going to have the time of my life all day long." Finally, he was to gather his little family about him and offer a prayer. "How," I asked, "do you expect to get anywhere without recourse to the Great Power?" But if he did not know a prayer, I suggested a very short one in affirmative form, one that I personally use every day and without which I just could not get along. "This is the day that the Lord has made; I will rejoice and be glad in it."

Well, as I say, my unenthusiastic writer friend listened to this whimsical sort of suggestion made to the audience in my talk. Afterward he confessed that at first it seemed a bit farfetched and a kind of put-on. But as he thought it over he realized that the decision to be negative or positive, glum or enthusiastic, was to be made in one's own thinking and action. "Believe it or not," he said a bit defensively, "I tried that crazy morning technique of yours and what do you know? It has already begun to work. Even my wife gets a big kick out of it. Says I'm different and a lot of fun. So I buy that 'as if' principle. I'm convinced that as I act out enthusiasm, enthusiasm does indeed return to me."

"Much Too Much" and Enthusiasm Drain-off

Some people who get into a hectic, "much-too-much" sort of living pattern complain that it's all so hard and demanding that enthusiasm is knocked right out of them. For example, I'm told that some wives seem to resent the term "housewife" as being in some way derogatory. They complain that housework—cooking, washing, cleaning—is drudgery and indeed a form of slavery imposed on them by male chauvinists. Of course such daily tasks can become tiresome, and with that we are sympathetic. But even the maternal instinct, the love and joy of caring for children, seems boring, not to the majority, of course, but still apparently to a fair number, judging from what I hear. And I've heard not a few husbands gripe about working around the house after coming home from a hard day at the office and having to "fix this" and "fix that." Many husbands work enthusiastically all day long, then come home and revert into gloomy negativists, making life miserable for hard-working wives.

Well, I know two couples who represent the opposite

ends of the enthusiasm spectrum, and both shall be nameless, for they wouldn't like this form of publicity. Strangely enough, each couple is approximately the same age and each has four boys, the last one just a baby. Of one complaining couple I asked, "How come you had these four boys if they annoy you so? What do you want—to be out dancing and partying every night? How about responsibility and maturity? Why all this playboy stuff?" I knew this young couple had quality of character; it just was not coming through at the time.

"Oh, it's all so lousy dull" was the reply. "It's just nothing but work, work, work, and noise and more noise. Haven't we got a right to our own lives?"

"But where is your enthusiasm for the wonderful and exciting opportunity to be parents and have a terrific family life with four growing boys? Just think of it—four of the most interesting characters in the world, four alive, healthy and vigorous boys."

"Okay, play it up as you will, but we have had just more than we can take." So ended an expression of futility at its insipid ultimate.

The second couple? Well, I met them in a restaurant recently. Daddy, it seemed, had taken Mommy out for dinner and they were both enjoying it, but obviously could hardly wait to get home to those four terrific kids.

"Bill and I have such an exciting time with our four boys. They are each different and so terribly interesting as personalities. Hasn't the Lord been good to us?"

"Come on, Jane, hurry with that chocolate mousse and let's get home. I promised to tell the boys that story about the magic airplane."

Let us hope the first couple gets turned on with enthusiasm for home and family before it's too late and the boys have left home emotionally marred. And let us

69

hope the second couple will never lose that top skill of successful living—to keep enthusiasm going.

Tiredness and Enthusiasm

Let's face it. Getting tired and worn out with unremitting demands exerts a strong draw against enthusiasm for all of us. The solution is to mingle interests into a creative life pattern. In the case of the second couple, they are both active in church work. The husband is a member of the board of deacons, the wife is superintendent of the beginner's department. She also takes leadership in a woman's club once a month, and he bowls every other week. They get out together for an occasional golf game. They are part of a couples group that meets around at homes with people who also have children. "Someday," said Jane, "I'm going to have a second career, but meanwhile my kids are my first career. And just in case you are wondering—yes, I feel liberated and very creative."

The other couple, the two people for whom enthusiasm had seemingly leaked away, had apparently been thus far unable to cope with the continuous demands of family life due to their value pattern, which gave precedence to social engagements. Theirs, it might seem, was primarily a priority problem and, not having worked out a balanced activity system, one that gave the parental function its due relationship to other aspects of life, they tended to react resentfully.

A new turn-on of enthusiasm could help give a more comprehensive mingling of interesting activities, which most well-organized and with-it people can effect. Indeed, organization itself contributes to the development of enthusiasm, and lack of it can produce the worn-out attitude that siphons off enthusiasm. It's not all that simple to get run down with weariness and at the same time stay up strong with enthusiasm. But as one seeks to do just that, hard or not, the result is greatly to diminish the weariness. Enthusiasm, in a deep sense and a solid one, is an energy-producer and, instead of reducing vitality, it tends to accentuate vitality due to its mental and emotional stimulation.

Tough blows coming one after another may understandably reduce the quality of living enthusiastically, at least temporarily, and if a person reacts in this manner, he is entitled to sympathetic appreciation of his problem. But still, the application of a solid and normal enthusiasm, despite a series of difficult experiences, can do much to nullify harsh effects and, indeed, to help the individual to rise above the blows he has suffered.

The ability to meet adversity and failure, sorrow and misfortune, with a smile and never to lose enthusiasm but to keep going at a high level is one of the most exciting demonstrations of the positive principle. But the persons who do this successfully and come through to new achievements are those who have something inside, something called faith and confidence and belief. They learn how to meet trouble with high heart. They never panic, but always keep thinking and probing for answers and for solutions. For them, a failure is but an incident in a success-motivated life; an incident from which they draw know-how and experience and added strength. Because always when you suffer a setback and overcome it, you emerge stronger than before. The following may be a bit grim as an illustration, but it makes a point: The American Indians once believed that when a brave scalped an enemy, the strength of that warrior passed into him. Many scalps of enemies meant more strength to the victor. It could be that the more big hardships you overcome, the stronger you are thereby.

People with enthusiasm of the self-repeating variety have an incalculable asset going for them, one that compensates for other deficiencies that they may possess. Some, for example, may be lacking in education, but if they have a vital and constantly revitalized enthusiasm, they ignore drawbacks and just go out and do a superior job. Like the story of "The New Salesman," which someone gave me not long ago:

> A new salesman wrote his first report to the home office and it stunned the brass to learn that obviously the "new hope" was a blithering illiterate. He wrote: "I seen this outfit which they ain't never bought a dime's worth of nothing from us and sole them a couple thousand dollars worth of guds. I am now going to Chicago." Before the illiterate could be given the heave-ho by his manager, another report came in: "I cum here and sole them a half-millyun." Fearful if he did and fearful if he didn't fire the peddler, the sales manager dumped the problem into the lap of the company's president. The following morning, members of the Ivory Tower were flabbergasted to see the two letters on the bulletin board and this letter from the president tacked above them. "We ben spending to much time trying to spel instead of trying to sel. Let's watch them sails! I want everybody should read them letters from Cooch who is on the rode and doing a grate job for us and should go out and do like he dun!"

"Things Are Terrific–Terrific"

W. Clement Stone, Chicago industrialist and philanthropist, began his life career at age six by selling newspapers on the South Side. By strong determination and positive thinking he became one of the top salesmen in this country. The more money he made (and he made plenty), the more he gave away to help poor boys and girls, to rehabilitate prisoners, to advance mental health, to strengthen religion, the arts and sciences. Indeed, the late Dr. Arnaud C. Marts, one of the greatest American fund-raisers for benevolent purposes, said, "Clem Stone is the most generous man I have ever known."

Mr. Stone sometimes overextends himself by giving so much that it threatens to impair his resources, and he, like all businessmen, suffers the ups and downs of the economy. But always he comes back, because he is a comeback sort of man.

Never in all the vicissitudes of his personal and business life have I ever known him to show one moment of depreciated enthusiasm. Whenever I have picked up the telephone and asked him how he is and how things are going, always in strong voice and strong spirit I have received the very alive answer, "Terrific, absolutely terrific!" Is this bravado or a superficial denial of trouble? Not at all. For this man knows the score. He is aware of difficulty, realistically aware. But the difference between Mr. Stone and some others is an interesting one. Mr. Stone likes success for the pleasure of succeeding, of overcoming difficulty. To him the resulting money is regarded as a tool by which to do good, raise the level of life, and motivate others to the potentials inherent within themselves. His enthusiasm is based on a burning desire to stimulate others to move up, always to move up.

As a result, in dark days as well as in sunny days, his reactions are always the same—terrific, terrific. He was turned on to enthusiasm as a ragged street urchin selling papers, and in a career of meeting roadblock after roadblock he has kept it going ever since. His method for doing this, as I have studied him, is never to react emotionally to what happens but always to look for and find in every circumstance the good that is surely present there. He believes that to every disadvantage there is a corresponding advantage. With this dispassionate attitude of cool, factual thinking, his batting average of successes over failures is remarkable. And the ability never to allow a setback to reduce enthusiasm has kept this man going, always going, through rough seas as well as calm waters. He is an outstanding example of the positive principle in action.

"He Turned Me On"

On an airplane I sat by a young man, an outgoing, interesting fellow. He told me that he had been a hostile kid on drugs and had always been dodging the police. Then he was induced to read a book by Mr. Stone.[9] For the first time in his mixed-up life this boy had a flicker of hope that he might become, as he put it, "a somebody." "That book turned me on, and I mean turned me on," he said in a voice that shook just enough to betray emotion. "I think I've got the enthusiasm to keep going no matter what tough breaks I may meet up with."

Personal Experience of Enthusiasm

I have my own method for getting turned on with self-repeating enthusiasm, and the procedure has worked well in my experience. Actually I'm sure that I have a greater enthusiasm now than at any previous time, and indeed it seems to increase in depth and quality. As a boy I was terrifically enthusiastic, but personal inner conflicts sometimes took the bloom off. Fortunately, that seems no longer a problem, for, having solved those conflicts, there remains little to interfere with a free flow of enthusiastic motivation.

[9]*The Success System That Never Fails*

This is not to say that there are no problems. Indeed, there are plenty of them, but finally I learned to tackle these difficulties with a positive assurance of dealing with them successfully. Naturally I have my "down" moments but not so many as formerly, nor do they last so long as they once did. This, of course, represents no perfection on my part. All it says, and believe me it is a lot, is that by the grace of God I finally found the answer to living a happy, exciting, and victorious life; and as a result learned how to get turned on with a self-repeating enthusiasm. So let me tell you how it came about for what it may be worth to you.

Back in 1932 I became minister of the Marble Collegiate Church on Fifth Avenue in New York City. For five years I had led a successful church in Syracuse where everything was going smoothly, indeed very well, and I myself was charged up with boundless enthusiasm. Then I received a call to this famous church. But things are not always the way they appear and I soon became aware that this church had problems. In fact, the congregation had dwindled to about two hundred persons. Sundays the big church was almost empty. It was the time of the Great Depression of the early thirties, and dollars were scarce. In Syracuse I'd had it good, something that certainly could not be said of this new responsibility.

Naturally I gave the job all I had of thought, energy, prayer, and indeed everything it takes to make things go, but they just did not go at all, or at the best, slowly. Every Sunday I looked out at rows of empty seats and big vacant balconies and from Monday to Saturday wondered where I was going to get the money to pay the bills.

After some months my energy began to run out. Mentally I became really discouraged and the natural enthusiasm which before had carried me over many a hurdle went down the drain. Finally I had to admit I'd about had it. I never quite came to the point of quitting, but still couldn't get much lower and really hit bottom. Then I learned a fabulous truth, a factor basic to the positive principle, that the bottom is really a great place. For when you hit bottom you've gone down as far as you can go. The only direction from there is up.

To get away for a vacation and hopefully a new perspective, my wife and I went to the Lake District in northern England. There I moped about daily pouring a lot of negativism into my poor wife's ears until finally she became fed up with it. She led me to a bench in a far corner of the beautiful garden of the hotel. She proceeded to imply that I was considerably less than a man to let my problems throw me, and how come I had the audacity to advocate a victorious way of life and at the same time be so defeated myself?

She then informed me, and gentle lady that she is she can be pretty tough, that I was going to remain on that bench until I had "turned my life with all of its problems over to God." While officially I was her pastor as well as her husband, she was taking over as my pastor. And believe me she knew how to handle a case like me. She told me what to do and how to do it.

Finally I prayed, at her direction, a simple prayer. It went something like this: "Dear Lord, I can't handle my life. My problems have me licked. I need help. So I turn my life over to You here and now."

This produced a strange and remarkable effect. It seemed that all dark thoughts immediately left my mind. A remarkable feeling of peace came over me. I now knew for sure that God and I together could handle that church. I found myself sort of walking on air. And the old enthusiasm and excitement came surging back! Plans and ideas and innovations bombarded my mind and I could hardly wait to get home to implement them.

I can honestly say that from that experience on a bench in that English garden until the present I have been turned on with self-repeating enthusiasm. Ruth and I have returned several times to sit on that bench. But a revisit hasn't been necessary really. It is only a sort of pilgrimage to a spot where something unforgettable happened. Find your own bench somewhere . . . but get turned on.

And that is a vital secret of successful living—to get turned on with self-repeating enthusiasm, in-depth enthusiasm, and to keep the positive principle going.

Let us recapitulate the methods for keeping enthusiasm operating at high level suggested in this chapter:

1. Study the source of enthusiasm of the ninety-year-old one-legged woman who accepted as fact the promise of abundant life.
2. Don't see yourself as old and getting older, as one who has just about had it because time has passed, even lots of time.
3. Live youthfully now—and always.
4. Never forget that all the enthusiasm you need is in your mind. Let it out—let it live—let it motivate you.
5. Practice thinking enthusiasm—practice turning your thoughts on to enthusiasm.
6. Act as if you had enthusiasm. Believe that you have it and you will be enthusiastic.
7. Never let the swamped feeling dampen enthusiasm. Keep the positive principle going with enthusiasm and nothing will ever be too much for you.

8. Cushion the painful effects of hard blows by keeping enthusiasm going strong, even if doing so requires struggle.

9. Always take the attitude that you can make things *terrific—terrific*—no matter the hazards. Indeed, the "terrific—terrific" attitude can nullify hazards.

10. Affirm enthusiasm—affirm, affirm, affirm.

FIFTH
WAY TO KEEP
THE POSITIVE
PRINCIPLE GOING

Drop Old, Tired, Gloomy
Thoughts and
Come Alive

New Year's Eve in Rome! It was really something and totally unlike anything we had previously experienced. As longtime residents of New York City, which can notably celebrate any event, nothing my wife and I ever witnessed at home could remotely compare with the turn-of-the-year observance in the Eternal City.

It all started about noon on December 31 with the booming of guns, a mounting crescendo of noisemakers; everywhere great reverberations. As night came on, tracer flashes cut the sky until finally at the stroke of midnight bedlam broke forth with cannonading from every quarter, underscoring the enormous concert of sound magnified and magnified. As we looked from the window toward the dome of St. Peter's with tracers leaping all about it, the effect was as if some huge army were attacking the city. (And the hotel manager told us that he had given us a quiet room!)

But this was not all. The Romans seem to have an idea that New Year's Eve is the appropriate time to rid themselves of the old and take on the new, not symbolically but practically, by throwing out of the window any old thing, such as a dress, a suit, cracked dishes, a dilapidated chair. Our Roman friends warned us to stay in our hotel to avoid the possibility of an old television set or something equally devastating bouncing off our heads.

The idea is a sound one not only for New Year's Eve but also every day, and the throwaway of the old might properly go far beyond unwanted objects to the disposal of all old, tired, gloomy thoughts. Every night before retiring, the ritual of mental thought-emptying will get the mind into good working order for the succeeding day. So every night deliberately drop those old, tired, gloomy thoughts and come alive.

Lesson From a Tailor

Years ago in Brooklyn I had a good friend who was also my tailor. When Mr. S. Pearson made a suit he also gave instructions for keeping it in good shape. "Every night at bedtime," he said, "remove everything from every pocket to prevent sagging of the garment." He then showed how to hang trousers with the lower part of one leg folded over the other on the hanger so that the trousers hung suspended, thus tending to eliminate wrinkles.

Like most men, I carry a wallet, a credit card case, keys, pencils and pens. I also carry with me miniature scissors for clipping out interesting articles. My pockets constitute a filing system for all sorts of notations and memos accumulated during the day and even some from days past. My pocket-emptying program stimulated the process of consolidating and laying those memos in one place. And what a pleasure to check off the ones that had been attended to, then to toss them one by one into the wastebasket. I put out on the dresser, along with keys, et cetera, notes to be handled tomorrow. The mass of reminders was in this fashion kept to a well-organized and manageable number and helped send me to bed with a mind at peace and a minimal feeling of guilt about things undone.

After performing this suit-emptying ritual for some weeks and experiencing the relief of dealing efficiently with notes and memos, the idea got through to me of employing the same procedure on the thoughts one accumulates, the worn-out attitudes, the gloomy impressions, regrets, discouragements with which the mind becomes cluttered. Accordingly, I began to bring up and do something about all the old, tired, dead, gloomy thoughts and consciously visualize them as passing out of consciousness, somewhat like watching them flow down a drain. I affirmed, "These thoughts are now flowing out of my mind—out of my mind. They are passing from me—passing, passing, now this very moment passing away."

Following this affirmation I employed the suggestion made by M. R. Kopmeyer in one of his books[1] relative to a quick falling asleep by "seeing" a dense fog swirling and spreading across consciousness, blotting everything out completely. I found that sleep was induced much more quickly by this procedure; thoughts that otherwise might have agitated the mind were lost in the heavy padded vagueness of that impenetrable fog which established an effective barrier between mind and the active world. The result was sound and restful sleep from which I awoke feeling a boundless sense of new life. This program helped reactivate the energy and vitality needed for each succeeding day. It became for me one viable method by which to keep inspiration going.

He Did a Job on His Thoughts

A man told me he was having a lot of trouble with himself. "You are not the only one," I reflected, thinking of

[1] *Here's Help!* P.O. Box 6302, Louisville, Ken. 40207.

the many letters I receive from people who ask for help with problems. And also thinking of myself; for I must admit that the person who has caused me the most trouble over the years has been Norman Vincent Peale. And most people will admit to the same, I believe, if they tell the full truth about themselves. If we are our own chief problem, the basic reason may be found in the type of thoughts which habitually occupy and direct our minds.

At least this was the conclusion reached by the man mentioned above. He was a person who genuinely desired to do a constructive job and he studied to perfect his work performance by attending professional seminars and sales motivational meetings. Also he was an avid reader of inspirational and self-help books. I came to know him when he wrote me after reading *The Power of Positive Thinking.* He was a sincere student who definitely worked at putting the book's principles into practice.

By such exposure he would in each instance become inspired and take on a strong, fresh motivation. But seemingly he could not hold his inspiration beyond a certain time frame. There would come a gradual reversal. Inspiration would start declining, excitement die down, energy lessen, motivation slow up. This process of motivational buildup and decline was repeated a number of times. He just could not seem to keep a positive mental attitude going without a reversal pattern taking place. When enthusiastically motivated he could sell very effectively and would move up into a higher echelon of opportunity in his organization. But when a decline in spirit attacked him, the decline in sales performance was in direct proportion to the falling off of his mental and spirit vibrancy.

This up-and-down reaction was naturally disturbing and he wrote at some length describing the mercurial nature of his responses. I suggested that he enter upon a course of psychological counseling. My personal opinion was that the problem lay somewhere in his intellectual-emotional balance system. But he lived some two thousand miles away, so I suggested that he get help locally, which he did to good effect.

In replying to his letter, apparently I unconsciously contributed a thought which may have turned the tide of his career. Somewhere a long time ago I read a quotation, for which I have never known the source, to the effect that "history turns on small hinges." Similarly, it may be assumed that the history of a personal life can turn on an offhand suggestion. In my message to him I quoted a line from the Bible: "Be renewed in the spirit of your mind."[2] This suggestion was made because of the fact that "running down" often originates in attitudes before it becomes evidenced in performance.

He Gets a New Spirit Going

Months later when I waited my turn to speak at a sales convention in the Rocky Mountain area, this man introduced himself, reminding me of his letter and my reply. He said that the statement from the Scriptures had done more to bring about a change in him than even the counseling sessions he had undertaken, which had been very helpful.

Just what does "renewed in the spirit of your mind" really mean? It puzzled our friend at first, but the idea really "grabbed" his thinking. He knew what was meant by team spirit, school spirit, company spirit—a kind of esprit de corps, a deep feeling interfused with loyalty and a carry-on-no-matter-what attitude. The process of thinking, he reasoned, was perhaps more than an intel-

[2]Ephesians 4:23.

lectual exercise. There had to be such a thing as a spirit in the mind, which must surely mean an emotionally tinged attitude of commitment, dedication, renewal—in a word, inspiration—which he now saw clearly meant to be inspirited or filled full of spirit. In other words, a liveliness that cannot be depressed but continues with vigor, whatever the circumstances.

"As a result of thinking along this line," he said, "I came up with four principles which enabled me not only to be motivated, but to keep that spirit of motivation going, unaffected by setbacks or resistances.

"1. At all times I had to maintain the 'keep-it-going' attitude.

"2. I had to cultivate my spirit quality to assure that I could sustain the 'keep-it-going' attitude in good days or bad.

"3. I had to renew myself on a spiritual basis if I expected to be renewed constantly in the spirit of my mind.

"4. I had to believe and affirm that nothing could anymore take the bloom off my spirit."

That these four principles had worked effectively in the personality and, consequently, in the career of this man was evident not only in attitude but also factually in his achievement record. "If you use this story," he cautioned, "I ask that my name not be mentioned, for I believe that my taking any credit for changing a spiritual basis of life can break the power flow, and the flow of spirit power is of first importance to me. Some amazing things started happening in my life and to me personally. Then changes came in my family and in my business when I really got down to it and did a job on my thoughts. But in the last analysis it was the revamping of the spirit that effected the greatest change in me and in everything with which I am connected," he concluded.

Love Cancels Out Gloomy Thoughts

In dropping old, tired, dead thoughts and coming alive I discovered early in my own personal experience that the simple practice of outgoing love toward people is almost magically effective. Whenever I detect that my thoughts are going stale, I deliberately search for some opportunity to express love by a thoughtful and kindly act, and if I do enough of this, a new vigor, even fervor, shows in my mental state. And along with it, a revitalized feeling of aliveness and sensitivity becomes evident. To me this practice is of tremendous importance.

Moreover, even a return in memory to personal experiences of proffered goodwill and compassion has the effect of washing out of mind the accumulation of old, tired, gloomy thoughts which constantly recur unless arrested by some stronger mental force. A powerful curative process of mental and spiritual attitudes is brought to bear by the infusion of caring thoughts followed by caring action.

I would like to relate three stories, all of them, strangely enough, associated with Christmases of other years. But each has lingered in mind, and while of course I try to do kindly deeds currently, the memory of the following very human incidents still possesses the power to help me drop the old, tired, listless or gloomy thoughts that, in all of us, are always endeavoring to take over our consciousness.

It Happened on a Cincinnati Street

Some of my most impressionable boyhood years were spent in Cincinnati, Ohio. I still remember the huge

Christmas tree in Fountain Square—the gleaming decorations, the frosty streets ringing with the sound of carols. Up on East Liberty Street where we lived, our mother and father always had a Christmas tree with real candles on it, magical candles which, combined with the fir tree, gave off a foresty aroma, unique and unforgettable.

One Christmas Eve when I was twelve, I was out with my minister father doing some late Christmas shopping. We were both loaded down with packages and I was getting tired of it and a bit cross. I was thinking how good it would be to get home, when a beggar—a bleary-eyed, unshaven, dirty old man—came up to me, touched my arm with a hand like a claw, and asked for money. He was so repulsive that instinctively I recoiled. Softly my father said, "Norman, it's Christmas Eve. You shouldn't treat a man that way."

I was unrepentant. "Dad," I complained, "he's nothing but a bum."

My father spoke strongly. "Maybe he hasn't made much of himself, but he's still a child of God." He then handed me a dollar—a lot of money for those days and certainly for a preacher's income. "I want you to take this and give it to that man," he said. "Speak to him respectfully. Tell him you are giving it to him in Christ's name."

"Oh, Dad," I protested, "I can't do anything like that."

My father's voice was firm. "Go and do as I tell you."

So, reluctant and resisting, I ran after the old man and said, "Excuse me, sir. I give you this money in the name of Christ."

He stared at the dollar bill, then looked at me in utter amazement. A wonderful smile came to his face, a smile so full of life and beauty that I forgot that he was dirty and unshaven. I forgot that he was ragged and old.

86

With a gesture that was almost courtly, he took off his hat. Graciously he said, "And I thank you, young sir, in the name of Christ."

All my irritation, all my annoyance faded away. The street, the houses, everything around me suddenly seemed beautiful because I had been part of a miracle that I have seen many times since—the transformation that comes over people when you think of them as children of God, when you offer them love in the name of a Baby born two thousand years ago in a stable in Bethlehem, a Person who still lives and walks with us and makes His presence known.

That was my Christmas discovery that year—the gold of human dignity that lies hidden in every living soul, waiting to shine through if only we'll give it a chance. Early in life I began to understand that the positive principle is deeply part of loving human relationships, and for that insight I am very grateful.

Drama at Life's End

The telephone call to my father came late at night, and from a most unlikely place—a house in what was called in those days the red-light district of the city. The woman who operated the house said that one of the girls was very ill, perhaps even dying. And the girl in her illness kept calling for a minister. Somehow the woman had heard of my father, pastor of a well-known church. Would he come?

My father never failed to respond to any human appeal. Quietly he explained to my mother where he was going. Then his eyes fell upon me. "Get your coat, Norman," he said, "I want you to come too."

My mother was aghast. "You don't mean you'd take a fifteen-year-old boy into a place like that!"

My father said, "There's a lot of sin and sadness and despair in human life. Norman can't be shielded from it forever."

We walked through the snowy streets and I remember how the Christmas trees glowed and winked in the darkness. We came to the place, a big old frame house. A woman opened the door and led us to an upstairs room. There, lying in a big brass bed, was a pathetic, almost doll-like young girl, so white and frail that she seemed like a child, scarcely older than I was.

Before he became a minister, my father had been a physician and he knew the girl was gravely ill. When he sat by her bed, the girl reached for his hand. She whispered that she had come from a good Christian home and was sorry for the things she had done and the life she had led. She said she knew she was dying and that she was afraid. "I've been so bad," she said. "So bad."

I stood by my father's side listening. I didn't know what anybody could do to help her. But my father knew. He put both his big strong hands around her small one. He said, "There is no such thing as a bad girl. There are girls who act badly sometimes, but there are no bad girls—or bad boys either—because God made them and He makes all things good. Do you believe in Jesus?" The girl nodded. He continued, "Then let me hear you say, 'Dear Jesus, forgive me for my sins.' " She repeated those words. "Now," he said, "God loves you, His child, and He has forgiven you, and no matter when the time comes, He will take you to your heavenly home."

If I live to be a hundred, I will never forget the feeling of power and glory that came into that room as my father prayed for that dying girl. There were tears on the faces of the other women standing there, and on my own, too. And everything sordid, everything corrupt, was simply swept away. Actually there was beauty in that place of evil. The love born in Bethlehem was revealing itself again in a dark and dismal house in Cincinnati, Ohio, and nothing could withstand it. It seemed to wash all evil from human hearts.

So that was the gift I received that Christmas, the frankincense-knowledge that there is good in all people, even the sad and the forlorn, and that no one need be forsaken because of past mistakes.

Unforgettable Christmas Eve

It was still another Christmas Eve, this time in Brooklyn, New York. I was feeling happy because things were going well with my church. As a young bachelor minister I had just had a fine visit with some friends and was saying good-bye to them on their front steps.

All around us up and down the street houses were decorated in honor of Christ's birthday. Suddenly a pair of wreaths on the house across the street caught my eye. One had the traditional red bow, bright and gay. But the ribbon on the other was a somber black—the symbol of a death in the family, a funeral wreath. It was the custom at that time and place to hang such wreaths outside a house of mourning.

Something about that unexpected juxtaposition of joy and sorrow made a strange and moving impression on me. I asked my host about it. He said that a young couple with small children lived in the house but he did not know them. They were new in the neighborhood.

I said good night and walked down the street. But before I had gone far, something made me turn back. I did not know those people either. But it was Christmas Eve, and if there was joy or suffering to be shared, my calling was to share it.

Hesitantly I went up to the door and rang the bell. A

tall young man opened it and spoke pleasantly to me. I told him that I was a minister whose church was in the neighborhood. I had seen the wreaths and wanted to offer my sympathy.

"Come in," he said quietly. "It's very kind of you to come."

The house seemed very still. In the living room a wood fire was burning. In the center of the room was a small casket. In it reposed the body of a little girl about six years old. Over the years in memory I can see her yet, lying there in a pretty white dress, ironed fresh and dainty. Nearby was an empty chair where the young man had been sitting, keeping watch beside the body of his child.

I was so moved that I could barely speak. *What a Christmas Eve*, I thought. Alone in a new neighborhood, no friends or relatives, a crushing loss. The young man seemed to read my thoughts. "It's all right," he said, as if he were reassuring me. "She's with the Lord, you know." His wife, he said, was upstairs with their two smaller children. He took me to meet her.

The young mother was reading to two small boys. She had a lovely face, sad yet serene. And suddenly I knew why this little family had been able to hang two wreaths on the door, one signifying life, the other death. They had been able to do it because they knew it was all one process, all part of God's wonderful and merciful and perfect plan for all of us. They had heard the great promise: "Because I live, ye shall live also."[3] They had heard it and they believed it. That was why they could move forward together with love and dignity, courage and acceptance.

The young couple asked if they could join my church. They did. We became good friends. Many years have

[3]John 14:19.

passed since then, but not one has gone by without a Christmas card from some member of that family expressing love and gratitude.

But I am the one who is grateful.[4]

And one chief reason that I am grateful is that these three experiences of expressed love did something unforgettable for me. They showed me one important method for constantly flushing from the mind the old, tired, gloomy thoughts that will surely accumulate there unless love and compassion displace them. This aspect of the positive principle has been of incalculable benefit.

Unhealthy thought patterns can block the flow of creative inspiration and inhibit the ability to function at maximum effectiveness. And there is perhaps nothing in life that may subject an individual to more intense torment than thoughts rooted in fear or hate or depressiveness. People in Bible times who were thus afflicted were said to be possessed of devils; demoniac possession, it was called. As mankind became more sophisticated, such notions came to be rather smiled at in amusement. But as people have become more educated, some scientists in human problems are persuaded that an individual can be possessed by what might be termed mental spirits that are so evil in the consequences they effect that perhaps the demon concept is not all that wide of the mark.

She Killed a Devil

That the positive principle working in the mind has a powerful effect in eliminating the devil of fear, one of the most devastating enemies of personal happiness and well-being, we see in the following letter:

[4]"I Remember Three Christmases," *Guideposts*.

Dr. Norman Peale:

I found your book "The Power of Positive Thinking" in a large box of books from a friend. It has
changed my life!

We live in a remote logging camp 35 minutes by air
from a small town.

The being afraid pressures were terrible. With four
very lively children under 9 years old, I was sometimes *very* scared and most of the time fearful. So
much so that I was on tranquilizers. Without them I
couldn't function, with them I could *just* get along.
I *knew* the plane wouldn't get our food or medicine in
to us. Or the children would get hurt or ill. Or the
snows would come early and the men would be off
work too soon.

When I started reading your book I hadn't done
anything to my house for over a week. So you can well
imagine what it looked like. All I could do was pace
the floor.

I could lose myself in a book if it was interesting
enough, and then I wouldn't worry. Your book was
the last one left in the box, as it looked far from
interesting; or strong enough to tame the savage
beast that was running rampant inside me.

It took me 3 days to read it. Which was a record, as
I usually finished a book an afternoon. I would try
the methods of all the people you wrote about. I was
frantic; none of them would work.

So I would read and try again. I felt my mind
running in circles, tighter and tighter ones too.

One morning I got up, took my pills (out of habit),
and realized I had slept through the night without
waking up. I had a terrific amount of hope. But I
knew I couldn't work up any Faith. By the end of the
day it dawned on me that hope was the underside of
faith, peace and joy the outside of it.

That night I didn't take any sleeping pills. Not
because of faith or hope, but because I forgot.

I had been hoping for an instant miracle. Now I
realize there has been a miracle. The miracle of
creation took seven days and the miracle of life takes

9 months. So even though it took longer than an instant, it is no less a mighty work of God.

I'm now not taking anything in the way of pills. Praise God!

For the first time in 6 months my house is clean, my hair is fixed, my nails manicured.

My husband is very proud of me and was teasing one night. He asked me if I had got a boyfriend. I told him I had. His name was Jesus.

Man in Hell

May I tell you another incident about one of America's most prominent writers, a longtime friend, who telephoned my office in the village of Pawling, New York, and abruptly began the conversation by saying, "I'm in hell."

"Where are you speaking from?" I asked, not quite convinced of the seriousness of the approach.

"Danbury, Connecticut," he replied.

"Now, look; Danbury [a city near to us] is not to be described in such a manner," I said. "It's a very nice town."

Somewhat exasperated, my caller declared, "The hell is not in Danbury; it's in me, right smack in my mind, and I'm sick and tired of it. May I come and see you?"

Such a request was not to be denied. Besides, I had great admiration for this man as a writing genius and affection for him as a friend.

He paced the floor of my office. "I can no longer write," he stormed. "I've lost the hang of it; no inspiration, no ideas, and no ability to express them even if I did have them. I feel dead. That's it—completely dead." I allowed him fully to ventilate his feelings, then reminded him that he had a superior mind and outstanding skill as a craftsman with ideas and the words to express them brilliantly. "But I can't think straight anymore because my mind is full of a mass of miserable thoughts that so plague me that creative thinking is just not possible."

"Okay," I said, "let's get it out. Let's have a real catharsis and mind-emptying and then a mind-cleaning. Come clean in our confidential relationship as a poor, mixed-up guy with a pastor. And don't fool around, for I will know if you are telling a phony story. The therapy will not work unless, with complete honesty, you unload all those sick thoughts that have taken over your mind and are destroying your happiness and, perhaps, you yourself in the process."

As he talked, a mass of fear and anxiety thoughts, interspersed with strong guilt reactions, spilled out in so continuous a stream that it evidenced a deep psychosis rooted, no doubt, in the unconscious area of personality. That this process brought temporary relief was obvious. But I suggested a course of in-depth counseling which he followed scrupulously over a period of time with the result that he was finally able to drop those old, dead, gloomy thoughts and come into a quality of aliveness that he had not known for many months. In fact, he exulted that he had never felt so alive. Moreover, he was able to keep his newly released mental powers going. "I killed that devil," he declared, "and got out of that hell, or maybe I should say that I got hell out of me. And am I happy! It was amazing how those old unhealthy thoughts had blocked off inspiration and brought motivation to a halt. I wouldn't have believed it possible."

But of course such complete renewal is possible. In fact, it is certain that the dropping or removal of old, tired, depressive or fear thoughts releases a strong flow of power through the mind. And when that exorcism happens, inspirational and motivational forces again operate unhindered. Such treatment, moreover, gives an individual a new grasp upon his control potential so that he is better able to keep the positive principle going regardless of whatever adverse circumstances may develop.

So when you have the problem of old, negative and gloomy thoughts, what steps may you take to overcome and correct the situation?

1. Vigorously cleanse out the old unhealthy thought pattern and dispose of it. And for good.
2. Take charge of your thoughts instead of allowing them to control you.
3. Every night empty your mind of unhappy thoughts as you empty your pockets.
4. "Be renewed in the *spirit* of your mind."
5. Do kindly things for people, for nothing can so completely erase gloom as the practice of caring and goodwill.
6. Kill your devil of fear, or inferiority, or whatever. Endure it no longer. Now—today—get rid of it for good and always. Admit it, face it, and with God's help act against it. You will win.

SIXTH
WAY TO KEEP
THE POSITIVE
PRINCIPLE GOING

Let Seven Magic Words
Change Your Life

Amazing indeed is the power of words or of word combinations to affect persons and situations. William Lyon Phelps, famed writer and professor of English, said that the ten greatest words in the English language are found in a familiar statement from *Hamlet*, "To be or not to be, that is the question." It can hardly be denied that those words do contain a solemn and far-reaching thought about personal destiny.

A well-known Shakespearean actor once declared that the greatest sentence is an eight-word line from an old spiritual: "Nobody knows the trouble I've seen, glory hallelujah!" That a victory over trouble, however gigantic, can be accomplished is certainly worthy of an alleluia!

I once spoke on the same program at a convention with a man who delivered a compelling talk in which he asserted that the success of any business or enterprise may be explained by a six-word formula. He traced the history of a number of businesses and showed how they owed their success to having carried out the creative idea in this six-word expression: "Find a need and fill it."

But there is a seven-word combination which has perhaps affected more people than any other statement ever made. It has demonstrated power to erase failure, increase strength, eliminate fear and overcome self-doubt. It will help any individual become a more successful human being in the top meaning of that term. Indeed, these seven words have the incredible power to make you everything you ever wanted to be when they are applied in depth. And that seven-word formula is this: "I can do all things through Christ. . . ."[1] If you are of other than the Christian heritage, simply change the words to read: "I can do all things through God." In those seven magic words is your formula for inspiration, power, motivation and the ability to keep it going —always to keep it going. Here is the positive principle in super-operative force.

How the Seven Magic Words Changed One Life

If you feel we are overstating the facts, or if you doubt the power of these seven words to change lives and motivate careers, read carefully the dramatic true story which follows. Then ponder the fact that whatever can happen to one person can happen to another.

One night a speech I was delivering in Danville, Virginia, was carried live on radio to a wide area in Virginia and North Carolina. In the latter state a young man, George Shinn, driving his car in the vicinity of Raleigh, tuned to the broadcast. It seemed to interest him and later he asked that our representative come to see him. Following that interview his executive assistant, C. L. Jenkins, inspected our Foundation for Christian Living, the headquarters of which is located at Pawling, New York. Mr. Jenkins gave a favorable report on the objectives and activities of this nonprofit religious enterprise

[1] Philippians 4:13

which distributes some 30 million items of Christian and inspirational literature yearly.

This was my introduction to George Shinn, an attractive young man, whose life story is a dramatic illustration of the manner in which religious commitment, strong motivation and innovative thinking can indeed make something remarkable of a human being.

A few years earlier Mr. Shinn and his mother were hard put to make ends meet. The father had died and the family was in debt. His mother, obviously a remarkable woman, pumped gasoline, was a check-out clerk in a supermarket, and worked as a telephone operator. George washed cars, worked in a bakery, later in a cotton mill. At one period he had to wear clothes other people handed down. These facts are stated here to indicate the degree of success later attained.

George graduated from high school, but his grades were "pretty low," he modestly remembers. It was necessary to attend summer school to secure his diploma. He realized, financially poor as he was, that he would need education, so he entered a business college, serving as janitor in lieu of paying tuition charges.

Janitor Moves Up

Then occurred one of those seemingly small happenings out of which big things grow, and because he knew how to handle this small matter he set the pace for greater things to follow. On a Saturday while engaged in his cleaning duties, two young women from out of town came in to inquire about the school, and George dealt with these prospective students. Unlike so many employees in business, he did not churlishly remark, "Don't you see the office is closed? This isn't my job. Come around on Monday. Don't bother me." That kind of reaction, the bench mark of the unsuccessful, never entered George's mind. He was proud of the school and showed the girls the classrooms, library and all the facilities and ended by signing them up as students, receiving their deposits. On Monday morning the boss changed his job from that of janitor to recruiter of students.

George became so successful in this activity that after his own graduation he continued in that capacity. The owner of the business college purchased other schools and in time offered George a partnership. Now he was on his way to success in business—a partner in six business colleges.

Disaster Strikes

The partnership perhaps expanded too rapidly and financial problems developed. The schools verged toward bankruptcy. George consulted a law firm, expert business advisers, and laid his papers before the heads of the firm and a certified public accountant. For several hours they studied his accounts and finally said, "We've got to give it to you straight. You'll have to give up. You haven't a prayer."

"No, no," George cried, "it can't be, it must not be."

Numbed, he headed along Interstate 85 driving almost unseeingly, eyes blurred with tears. The tar strips in the road seemed to thump out the dismal refrain, "Failure! Failure! Failure!" Overwhelmed by these thoughts of failure, he pulled off the road and sat slumped over the wheel. "You haven't a prayer—you haven't a prayer." The words of the lawyer hammered into his brain. And when a brain gets hammered, it often opens up some new and powerful insight, which is precisely what happened in this instance.

Suddenly a terrific thought flashed up. "Why, I *do* have a prayer! Of course I have a prayer, but not like the lawyer meant it. Prayer is my hope, prayer is my answer." So he prayed a simple prayer but a powerful one, powerful because he meant it completely, and it activated amazing results. "Dear Lord," he said humbly, "I never was very bright but I do so much want to be a creative person. I want to be somebody and do things to help people. I give my life into Your hands to guide and direct me." Then he added this pertinent promise, which was to change him from a failure to a success: "Dear Lord, if You will do the thinking, I will do the work. Amen."

Every day affirming the seven magic words, George went at his problems with new confidence and increasingly constructive thinking. He began reorganizing his schools and expanding the curriculum. People came to his aid with refinancing when they saw that he was sincerely trying to render a constructive service. And besides that he had unquestioned ability.

Dramatic Recovery

Now he had developed a strange new capacity of mind and spirit. He became an inspiring and effective leader in the industry. Enrollment grew, new schools were added to his chain of educational institutions. As expertise increased, other schools throughout the country started coming to him for consulting services. Today the once nearly bankrupt organization has over five thousand students, with a staff of six hundred, and serves as management consultants to over forty other business and junior colleges. While the schools are profitable, their earnings are relatively modest compared with the profits created by other businesses operated by George Shinn & Associates—a consulting agency, an automobile leasing firm, an insurance business, a dealership in furniture and equipment, and so on.

Shinn, a confirmed tither, gives more than 10 percent of his income to religious work. He and his wife and children live modestly. He is himself a down-to-earth person, taking his rapid success at age thirty-four with simplicity and humility. Recently a recipient of the distinguished Horatio Alger Award given to persons who have attained outstanding success from lowly beginnings, he sincerely gave the credit, in his case, to "God working in my life." He speaks frequently in churches and to various types of organizations, in each speech telling of "the miracles God performed" in his experience, a partnership in which "the Lord does the thinking and I do the work." His foundation gives generously to the education of pastors through scholarship aid, and to other religious enterprises, including the Foundation for Christian Living.

Some may possibly regard such outgoing religious commitment as admirable but still a bit odd for a successful businessman. But Shinn is far from being odd. He is a normal American boy who grew up in difficult circumstances but who had the motivation to build a creative life. That dynamic motivation came through intense prayer in a time of looming failure. As a result he "committed everything to the Lord" and put his faith in the seven magic words. Mr. Shinn's experience demonstrates that anyone who fully embarks on such a program can indeed accomplish outstanding achievements.

We do not have to be failures. We were not born to fail; we were born to succeed. The secret of so doing is to drop the negatives and the excuses. Get going with a God-directed program, adopt a policy of giving, believe in hard work plus consistent application of the positive principle, and any person can become what he wants to be. He will reach his goal if he wants to badly enough.

Trust Yourself

"Self-trust is the first secret of success" is an oft-quoted remark attributed to Ralph Waldo Emerson. By the in-depth practice of the seven magic words one finds that he can, indeed, "do all things." Then that person is on the way to developing the most important of all success qualities—self-trust and self-belief. One thing is sure: The road to success is never via a supine self-doubt or a weasel inferiority complex. Success requires a humble yet real sense of adequacy, a normal self-respect, and with it the conviction that you can accomplish what you want to do.

Virgil, wise man of antiquity, said, "They can because they think they can."[2] And Goethe agreed with this vital principle by saying, "As soon as you trust yourself you will know how to live."[3] The practice of the seven magic words leads to a normal and sound trust in oneself and to a belief in the quality and integrity of one's own personality.

An Australian newspaper carried a fascinating story about a friend of mine, Sir John Walton, of Sydney.[4] The article stressed the place of positive thinking and faith in the remarkable career of Sir John, who once told me that in his early life he was plagued by insecurity feelings and suffered from a failure pattern. The newspaper, describing the career of this illustrious retail business leader, made reference to an effective sixteen-word spiritual formula in developing attitudes that helped him to keep motivation going to a high level of successful achievement:

[2] *The Aeneid.* Bk. 5.
[3] *Faust.* Pt. 1. Apprentice Scene.
[4] *Sun-Herald* Sydney.

The 71-year-old retail tycoon this week announced his retirement after 45 years of "working flat out."

The man who started on a shilling a week as a shop boy in a factory believes there is still room at the top for the self-made man.

"I can't see anything to stop a man from pulling himself up by his bootstraps if he's prepared to pay the price," Sir John said.

"I think there are always opportunities to make it, but I believe the vast majority of people are not really trying their hardest; they give up when the going gets tough.

"You have to work long hours, strive hard and apply yourself to the limit before you achieve your goal," he said.

"I once read a book called *The Power of Positive Thinking*, by Dr. Norman Vincent Peale.

"I was so impressed I attended his church in New York to hear him lecture.

"He was talking about faith, using the Biblical text, 'If ye have faith, as a grain of mustard seed, nothing shall be impossible unto you' [Sir John's sixteen-word formula].

"That's been my philosophy ever since—you can do anything if you have faith in yourself.

"That's why I carry a mustard seed token to remind me that I can do anything I want to," he said.

But things have not always been easy for Sir John.

In his soft spoken voice he recalled how he did badly at school, found it hard to keep a job and concentrated on enjoying himself.

"Until I was 26 I just drifted along with the tide," he said.

"I had a succession of jobs but couldn't keep them for long.

"Then I took stock of myself, gave up drinking and smoking, and joined the National Cash Register Company as a salesman."

He went on to become manager for New South Wales and, later, Australian managing director.

"This is going to sound terribly pompous but my

success didn't surprise me," he said.

In 1951, with the help of two former NCR directors, Sir John bought Murdoch's—the rundown menswear store that was to become the first link in one of the biggest retail chains in Australia.

The mammoth American retailer, Sears Roebuck, was impressed by the rapid growth of the company and invested in its future.

In 1970 John Walton was knighted by Queen Elizabeth II.

Believe in Yourself

Sir John Walton had to learn, as a faltering and stumbling young man weighed down by a hindering inferiority complex, that he must believe in himself and trust himself if he expected to realize his hopes and dreams. He did find himself through the philosophy and faith contained in positive Scriptural teachings. His career illustrates the truth that as a person learns to believe in God and to trust Him in everything, fully and completely, he also learns to believe in and trust himself. And this is a logical sequence, for every individual created by God has something of God-quality within him which positive faith can release.

Some people falsely, I believe, argue that believing in God and then believing in one's self is somehow "using God" to advance one's own interests. But as I view the matter, an urge, impulse or motivation has been built into an indivudal by the Creator to do the best possible with himself in this world. This does not mean, of course, that he should attempt to achieve his goals at the expense of others. It means simply that a basic force operating in human nature is the Divine Nature, which in turn means that we are designed to possess the self-confidence necessary for meeting tests and responsibilities.

Since a book is to some extent a documentary on the author's experience, I must confess that one of the chief problems I had to deal with was developing self-confidence. I have often declared that mine was the most enormous inferiority complex ever born in the state of Ohio, my native state. I was shy, reticent, scared, retiring and bashful. The word "bashful" is seldom used in current speech but is a highly descriptive term meaning, literally, to be abashed. Just about everything floored me.

Curiously, despite these pathetic inferiority feelings, I always wanted to become a public speaker. I was impressed when I heard some of the great speakers of that day, political figures like Theodore Roosevelt and William Jennings Bryan, and outstanding preachers—all great masters of public assemblage. I wanted to be like them. In that era there were many notable orators in the pulpit and on the platform. Perhaps it was the golden age of great public speaking. This was a period in American history when there was a galaxy of men who had a genius, hardly seen since, to sway vast audiences by their eloquence. It was thrilling to hear them, and to a small, scared boy with an inferiority complex they were heroes worshipped from afar.

Once in Greenville, Ohio, Williams Jennings Bryan, one of the greatest public speakers this country ever produced, three times a candidate for president, came to town. He spoke from an improvised platform set up on the high school grounds and surrounded by a huge crowd from all the countryside around. Another kid, as shy as I, joined me in an effort to be tough and swaggering, a common form of compensation for inferiority. We got a big cigar, cut it in two, and crawled under the speaker's platform for a clandestine and first smoke. After a few puffs I became sick, and I mean sick, so much so that it finished me on smoking. To this day I can recall lying on the ground under that platform while the great man stomped and thundered above me. My bravado faded and back I went to that shy state of being like a scared rabbit.

Learned the Self-Confidence Secret

My father was an outstanding speaker widely sought after in Ohio for all kinds of events. Once he offered a prayer at the State Republican Convention in Columbus and waxed so eloquent as he described the stirring events of American history and the great leaders (all Republicans) which it produced that when he said "Amen," the audience burst into thunderous applause. The chairman of the meeting said it was "the greatest speech ever delivered to a political convention in Ohio." But my father humbly reminded him that the speech was delivered to God as a prayer.

At any rate, my father understood my dream of becoming a public speaker and strongly empathized with my nervousness and shyness, for he had experienced the same feelings in his younger days. He taught me first that a speaker must have a message in which he thoroughly believes; and he must be completely sincere, for if there is anything phony his insincerity will come through loud and clear. He also taught me that a truly great speaker must love people and want to help them. To be effective, he must talk to people in their own thought and language forms, using illustrations with which they can identify. He used the figure that even as a mountain gathers up moisture and sends it back upon the countryside as rain, so the great speaker gathers up the hopes, dreams and needs of the people and sends back upon them inspiration to help them realize those values which they seek.

My father realized that he had a problem in the acute inferiority attitudes of his son and that it would do little good to suggest that the boy take himself in hand, start believing in himself and stand up like a man instead of crawling like a worm. Having been a physician before he became a preacher, and having learned from both disciplines a subtle understanding of the effect of subconscious attitudes in determining personality reactions, my father was aware that only an in-depth revision could give me self-confidence. He handled the self-defeating attitudes of his young son carefully and with skill. Over months he spelled out the fact that only a basic change in the boy's nature could bring about release from the hold upon him of inferiority and inadequacy feelings. Never did he employ such superficial methods as to say, "Buck up, be a man. Don't crawl through life cringing like a coward." No, my father was too smart for that. He simply encouraged me to hope that there was an answer, a way to change, and gradually he led me to it.

He Taught the Seven Magic Words

One beautiful summer Sunday after church my father took me for a long walk in the country near Greenville, where we lived. We tramped for several miles over meadows, along a peaceful country road and through the woods. I recall with fond memory that we stopped at a farmhouse to say hello to a family, members of his church. They brought out cold glasses of milk, cookies and some of the most delicious homemade ice cream I ever put in my mouth. So wonderful was it that this moment remains forever unforgettable.

It was twilight as we turned toward home, having some five or six miles to walk. As the sun was sinking lower in the west and the sky lighted up in sunset glory, we sat to rest on two stumps, looking out over the fields of Darke County, one of the richest agricultural lands in America. Dad said, "Norman, may I say that only Jesus Christ can change your life. If you will put yourself in His hands, He will take from you all fear, all self-doubt, all of those miserable inferiority feelings. He will make you confident and strong. If you want to be a public speaker, able to touch and move the minds and hearts of men and women, let Jesus take charge of your own mind and heart. And the time to do that is now, here with your father who loves and believes in you." So saying, he, in the old-fashioned way, knelt by the stump on which he had been seated; and I, too, knelt, and he committed me to Christ.

"Now," he said as we walked down the lane toward our little house, "always remember this truth—with Christ as your Helper you can be confident and strong and live a great life. Remember and never forget that the seven magic words will change your life: 'I can do all things through Christ. . . .' "

Father was a wonderful man, a man's man, a great and unusual personality. He has been gone a good many years from this world, but actually he lives and always shall live for me, for he taught me that summer afternoon the meaning of strong and loving fatherhood and then he led me to the Source of confidence.

The years have been many since that Sunday afternoon walk, but even now when the old self-doubt tends to grab me again, I hear over the mists of time my father's voice in the dear old familiar accents saying, "Don't be afraid; remember the seven magic words." Today my schedule has me speaking to some large audience on an average of three or four times weekly in every section of the United States and Canada and even overseas. But every now and then, there is a moment just as I am being introduced when the old fear crops up, the fear that I cannot do it; the old self-doubt tries to take over. Then I remember my father, who still guides his son, saying, "You can do all things through Christ." So I put my faith in Him and do the best I can. I owe an enormous personal debt of gratitude for the seven magic words which changed my life and which guide my life every day.

Seven Magic Words in Time of Crisis

People are called upon to face crises and difficult situations and here again the seven magic words supply the strength required under such circumstances. The promise that "I can do all things through Christ . . ." has probably pulled more persons through more difficulties than almost any other ever made. Like the man I met on a street with whom I talked for perhaps five minutes. He stopped me to say that he had been "passing through deep, dark waters," to use his own dramatic phrase. Standing alongside the flow of traffic, both motor and pedestrian, he recounted the mass of difficulties pressing upon him. His wife was in the hospital for an operation. He had just received a cut in salary. A teen-age son was in trouble with the law. He was finding it hard to pay his bills. "One thing after another," he said, and added, "isn't it strange how troubles seem to come in bunches all at one time?"

I started to outline methods for handling his problems but he stopped me. "Don't be concerned," he said. "I just took this advantage of meeting you to open my heart a bit. But actually I'm on top of things. Nothing can really get me down, and it will all come out okay." Standing on that street I heard them again—the seven magic words—and never did they sound more dramatic.

never did they seem more real, than when this hard-hit man said with positive assurance, "I can do all things through Christ. . . ." He had what is required to keep going.

Still another evidence of the power of these tremendous seven words came to me in a speaking tour among American servicemen in Vietnam at a time when that war was at its height. I was at an outpost to speak at a memorial service for a marine division on Hill 44. A number of men had lost their lives and their comrades were gathered for a solemn service in memory of them. It was an unforgettable experience to address some seven hundred men far up in the battlefront on an occasion which deeply moved all of us.

Before the meeting I had a few minutes with a group of chaplains. One of them, a Roman Catholic priest, had to leave to travel some miles to give Communion to men occupying an extremely dangerous forward position. To reach these few men, the chaplain himself would be forced to pick his way through mine fields, always in danger of stumbling upon a land mine that could destroy him.

"Did you volunteer for this kind of duty, Chaplain?" I asked.

"Yes," he replied.

"And why?" I prodded.

"Why?" he echoed. "Why, because I am a servant of our Lord and those men are His children. They are His sheep and I am His shepherd."

I was deeply moved by the simple sincerity of this dedicated man who was willing to put his life on the line for the "sheep," namely, lonely American boys in a deadly danger spot. "Must take a lot of courage," I commented with genuine admiration.

His answer was classic. "Oh, I don't know. I just depend upon the help that will always come to me." He hesitated, then added, "He has never let me down and He never will, no matter what happens." So saying, he walked out in the direction of danger, possibly even death. I was profoundly affected by this man and his faith. He rested everything upon the seven magic words. He had an inspiration and a powerful motivation to help men and serve God. And with it he possessed the power to keep it going. The positive principle was his way of life.

And now a recapitulation of the ideas presented in this chapter:

1. The power of words to change your life comes to top helpfulness in the seven magic words: "I can do all things through Christ. . . ."
2. The seven words can help you to overcome any defeat.
3. Never think you "haven't a prayer." You *do* have a prayer to carry you through.
4. Spiritual commitment is not for oddballs but for "with it" people.
5. Confidence and self-trust are by-products of the seven magic words.
6. Let self-confidence knock out your inferiority complex.
7. In crisis let the seven words take over. They will carry you through anything, everything.
8. You are always watched over in danger.
9. Live by the faith that will never let you down.

SEVENTH
WAY TO KEEP
THE POSITIVE
PRINCIPLE GOING

You Can Do Wonders If
You
Keep Trying

If you really try, you can—! That is right, the things that
you now think have you defeated, licked, beaten—those
things can be handled, dealt with, overcome. And how?
Just simply by *trying*. Only a minuscule few of those who
accomplish things in this world are in any sense super-
intellects. However, they have one super quality that
keeps them going: They just plain try. You'll never
know what you can do until you try—just try. Indeed,
that is the name of the game.

The attitude taken toward problems and difficulties is
far and away the most important factor in controlling
and mastering them. The motivational writer Kermit W.
Lueck[1] reports on a university research program which
was set up to determine the factors in the formula for
success. They are listed as four in number: I.Q., knowledge, skills and attitude. And according to Lueck, attitude accounts for an astonishing 93 percent of success.
Of primary importance is the I-will-keep-trying attitude, the never-give-up, the stick-with-it, the hang-in-
there, the keep-it-going attitude.

[1] *This Is Your Life*
One Small Step, One Giant Leap–Goals, distributed by Self Image Products, Inc.

My Mother Made Us Try

My mother was a sweet and gentle lady. But she could be a very strict disciplinarian, for there was one thing she would never permit her children to do and that was to quit. I can still hear her strong voice, firm and clear, saying, "Remember this and never forget it—the Peales never quit." She deliberately tried to build tenacity and dogged perseverance, undeviating persistence, into the fabric of her children's minds.

Of all subjects in school, the most difficult for me was mathematics. I liked English and history, studied them faithfully and enthusiastically, but must admit I tried to goof off, shall I say, on math. But would my mother let me get away with that? Hardly! "You can get it if you will just try and try again, and keep on trying," she insisted, and added, "You might as well get busy and master it because I personally am going to make you keep trying until you do." Well, my mother's wise discipline paid off, for while, of course, I have never been offered a professorship in mathematics, I did learn one vital lesson to the effect that if you simply try, you have learned one of the greatest of all success secrets.

Actually, those who perfect the "try" technique may not be endowed with brilliant talent, but they go places in life, sometimes even to the attainment of stellar achievement, because they become indomitable and undefeatable competitors. It becomes utterly impossible for them to accept the mediocre or to cease from striving for seemingly elusive perfection.

Ty Cobb—Always the Competitor

The late Branch Rickey's fine documentary on our long-time national game[2] is a classic of its kind, especially in

[2]*The American Diamond* New York: Simon and Schuster.

its appraisal of the great athletes in baseball history and the qualities that make a top baseball player.

Rickey's choice for the two greatest players of all time, at least up to his day, were Honus Wagner, famous shortstop of the Pittsburgh baseball club, and Ty Cobb, the immortal Georgia Peach of the Detroit club. He calls Cobb, "the choice of that *one* player for that *one* game that *had* to be won." Rickey says that Cobb did not have a great arm; so to compensate, he practiced almost by the clock in throwing from the outfield. His object was to have the ball skip when it hit the ground on its first contact and not to bounce with retarded speed. That meant definite control of the spin and the proper trajectory. "Did anyone," asked Rickey, "ever hear of a baseball player who voluntarily and alone would impose upon himself such arduous practice? As a result, he developed an accuracy, elevation of the throw and right rotation which made him the greatest of all fielders."

Cobb never took a double step on his throw from the outfield. He threw right where he caught the ball. He had figured that "the runner is moving at full speed and will run fifteen feet while I am stepping five." He became the terror of base runners because he always tried to make himself as near-perfect a baseball machine as possible. Rickey calls him "baseball's most earnest and assiduous learner—the greatest perfectionist both on offense and defense." He had a lifetime batting average of .367 and the almost incredible record of 892 stolen bases.

Zig Ziglar is a popular motivational speaker at sales meetings. In his fascinating book *See You at the Top*,[3] he tells a story about Ty Cobb that further illustrates the "always try" principle which went into the making of this immortal figure of baseball. When Cobb got on first

[3]We Believe, Inc., Dallas, Tex. 75251.

base he had an apparently nervous habit of kicking the bag. It wasn't until he retired from the game that the secret came out. By kicking the bag hard enough Cobb could move it a full two inches closer to second base. He figured that this improved his chances for a steal or for reaching second base safely on a hit. Compete, compete, compete—this is the keep-it-going spirit by which the person who tries will ultimately make records.

Trying, of course, cannot be for a time only but, rather, must be a continuous process constantly sustained at high level. When this is done, then in due course the goal will be achieved, the objective attained. Continue, continue, continue, is a three-point formula for success. The pity of it is, however, that all too many individuals do not continue long enough but instead become tired or discouraged or overcome by a sense of futility.

So they simply chuck the effort and cease trying. "It's no use, I'm going to skip it." So saying, they embrace the ultimate failure. They simply quit. But often, had they continued the effort just a bit longer, the thing for which they had given so much effort would have been attained. How pathetic, just to up and quit when, unbeknownst, the objective was about to be accomplished. Dr. V. Raymond Edman quotes William J. Cameron as saying, "The last dejected effort often becomes the winning stroke."[4]

Somewhere I heard a story of a prospector for gold in the old days out West. For days he had driven his pick into the earth looking for a vein of gold which he was sure was there. Day after day he swung his pick and sweated in the process. But finally the virus of discouragement got to him. With one angry and futile gesture he drove the pick into the ground, gathered up his gear

[4]From V. Raymond Edman, Ph. D., "The Disciplines of Life."

and went away. Many years later the pick, now rusted, the handle rotted away, was found just six feet from a rich vein of gold. Persist, hang in there, keep it going —that is the answer. That is the positive principle that gets results, reaches objectives, gains goals.

But How Do You Keep It Going?

To manage the problem of long and arduous sustained effort, it is important to harness the power of imagination, the technique of imaging. Form a mental picture or image of the goal you wish to attain and another picture of that goal as now in the process of being achieved, and you have put wings under the hard toil of trying.

For example, you want a beautiful home. How will you go about getting it? By saving and by hard work, of course. But that can become a long and hard process that may take the enthusiasm out of your effort. Therefore, form a picture in your thoughts of that house as already built. There it stands, with lawns, trees and flowers surrounding it. You can almost hear the key turn in the lock as you make ready to enter. Always realizable objectives are formed mentally before they are actualized in fact.

There was the man in New York City who was motivated by one of my talks to go ahead with a business he had long wanted to undertake but had delayed in starting because of the hesitant feeling that he couldn't make it go. Once encouraged to start, he found the going slow and difficult. He was a persistent character and he worked long and hard, but that he was beginning to tire and run out of enthusiasm became increasingly evident. Then we had a talk in which I outlined what Maxwell Maltz used to call "the imagineering principle." I suggested that he begin at once to activate imagination and to image successful outcomes, to see his business as turning in one success after another and achieving good results. He proved to be an excellent student of scientific truth principles, for he began affirming the best, visualizing the best and soon was having one best after another occurring in his business enterprise.

Prayerize, Visualize, Energize, Actualize

It was more than interesting, actually even inspiring, to observe this man as he employed dynamic visualization techniques which, when coupled with assiduous attention to the business and long hours of work, plus concentration, began to produce definitive results. He moved steadily onward toward the creation of a successful enterprise out of humble beginnings. When he had brought the business out into the clear as a proven achievement, he explained that a four-point formula was responsible for his success. And that formula was (1) Prayerize, (2) Visualize, (3) Energize, (4) Actualize. By that curious explanation he meant, of course, that he received guidance and strength through prayer. Then he developed a mental picture or image of his undertaking as already demonstrating success. Then he gave it sustained energetic activity. And finally, his experience once again proved that images strongly held in consciousness, when supported by the trying principle vigorously applied, will indeed actualize into solid results. He was able not only to develop dynamic motivation but also to keep that motivation going through the varied difficulties which confronted him.

The *prayerize, visualize, energize* and *actualize* procedure exerts a profound power force in the experience of the individual who has the wit to employ it. Roy Burkhart lived by this creative principle and it was responsible for seemingly incredible success outcomes for him. One experience may serve as an example of the astounding thought system which characterized his outstandingly successful life. On one occasion he put on a campaign in his home city of Columbus, Ohio, for an organization called World Neighbors, of which my friend John Peters is now the head. The function of this organization is to develop a caring concern for the less fortunate. Roy Burkhart staged a huge meeting in the old Memorial Hall in Columbus and invited me to be the speaker. He exultantly declared he was imaging a remarkable outpouring of neighborliness at this meeting.

The Hall Is Full

I arrived in Columbus at about two o'clock on the day of the meeting in a driving downpour of rain. The meeting was scheduled to begin at 8 P.M. Sodden skies overhead promised continuous rain and it was coming down in sheets as I dashed from the airplane into the airport building. There I met Roy, who had a most enthusiastic smile on his face. "Great to see you!" he declared, grabbing my hand. "Sure is good to have you in Columbus. The hall is full, the hall is full."

"What do you mean, 'The hall is full'?" I asked, bewildered. "Do you mean to tell me that a three-thousand seat auditorium is full at 2 P.M. on a soaking rainy day for a meeting scheduled to begin six hours from now?"

"The hall is full," he repeated, "full up to the top balcony, and everything is all set for a terrific meeting." Then I understood. The hall was full in his mind. He had a mental picture of a full house and of an enthusiastic capacity crowd.

At 7:45 P.M. I arrived at the hall on Broad Street in a wild, wind-driven rainstorm. About half soaked, I walked onstage and what did I see? A capacity crowd, every seat taken and people standing. I looked at Roy's beaming countenance. Was he surprised? Not at all. He had imaged it, pictured it, seen it in advance. Then I realized that before the actual hall was full it had been full in the mind of a man who had prayerized, visualized, energized, by working his head off and it was actualized into a fact. And so impressed was I that never to this day have I ceased to be amazed by the strange and marvelous power of "imagineering" that puts wings, powerful uplifting wings, under the try-and-keep-on-trying principle. Ever afterward when any difficulty arose, I would remember Roy and "The hall is full," and so I became better able to keep the positive principle going.

The visualization technique depends for its validity upon careful and thorough study, upon the application of diligent activity and effort. But always there must be involved a mental attitude of intelligent and positive faith if the forces of success are to be activated into a process of achievement. Of all such forces, the most basic and the most powerful is that of imagination, or the exercise of the viable and effective image.

Visualizes Himself as Winner

It happened at the Bellerive Country Club in St. Louis, scene of the 1965 United States Open Golf Championship competition. Posted on the large leader board were the names of the greats in golf, all winners of previous U.S. Opens.

A man stood looking up at that board with its list of distinguished winners. The last name was Ken Venturi, who had won the coveted prize the year before. There was a blank space reserved for the as-yet-unknown champion for 1965. But the man gazing at that leader board, a golfer from South Africa, saw a name in that blank space. And the name he saw was his own—Gary Player.

He had already won the British Open in 1959, the prestigious Masters in 1961, and the coveted PGA cup in 1962. But until now the U.S. Open had been elusive. When Gary Player took that stellar competition, he would become the third man to win the "Grand Slam" of golf, the two others being Gene Sarazen and Ben Hogan, immortal figures in the realm of golf.

In his thrilling book,[5] the first chapter of which is called "Visualize Winning," Gary says, "I saw something no one else could see." He writes:

> All week long I had been reading and studying *The Power of Positive Thinking* by Norman Vincent Peale, and what he had to say made a lot of sense to me. His words "visualize winning" were etched deeply in my mind. This had been my pattern for many years, but now the techniques for visualizing a goal emerged in concrete form.
>
> In spite of the intense heat I played very well. After fifteen holes my lead over Kel Nagle had lengthened to three strokes. I recall walking down the 15th fairway with Mr. Hardin of the United States Golf Association and that he said, "Well, you've got it all locked up." And I remember replying, "No, you can never say that until the last putt has been holed." I was so right!
>
> On 16 my 4-wood off the tee nosed right into a bunker. Somehow this seemed to trigger disaster, and before finishing the hole I'd taken a double bogey. And to make matters worse, just as I walked off the green, the news squawked through the walkie-talkie that Nagle had birdied 17. My three-stroke lead had dissolved, and now we were even. The heat was on and I knew it.
>
> But as I concentrated, the positive side of my mind began to take over. I had to have a par on 18 to stay

[5]*Gary Player, World Golfer* by Gary Player with Floyd Thatcher, copyright © 1974. Used by permission of Word Books, Publisher, Waco, Texas.

even with Kel, but a birdie would give me the one-stroke lead needed to win. Why not try for it?

The 18th at Bellerive is a tough par-4—trees on the left, out of bounds on the right. My drive landed in excellent position on the right side of the fairway, and a 5-iron second shot came to rest on the green just fifteen feet from the hole. Then came that big moment of truth. After studying the greens, I sighted the putt carefully, and then . . . it moved right along a line directly toward the cup but faltered to a stop just a fraction short. It's true golf is a game of inches, but this was unreal.

. . . My easy tap-in insured a tie with Nagle at 282—two strokes over par—and we were headed for an 18-hole playoff the next day. *Visualize winning?* I still was, but it would have to wait.

I went into the next day's round feeling good and hitting well. After four holes I was leading Nagle by one stroke. The pressure he felt as he teed up for number 5 must have been tremendous, for disaster struck. Kel's drive arced badly and bopped a woman spectator right on the head. Blood poured from her scalp as she toppled over unconscious. I tried to reassure Kel: "Don't let it get you." But obviously shaken and unnerved, he moved up to the ball again and this time blasted a grass-cutter that ricocheted off another woman's ankle. The remaining thirteen holes slipped by without much excitement, at least when compared to number 5.

The results after eighteen holes: Player, 71; Nagle, 74. The United States Open, America's biggest golf championship, was mine. . . all mine. It had not been won by a foreign player since Ted Ray captured the title in 1920—forty-five years before.

With this win I had joined ranks with Gene Sarazen and Ben Hogan. Now there were three members of the gilt-edged Grand Slam club . . . and I was one of them. This had to be one of the happiest moments of my life.

So at last the name of Gary Player went up on that leader board where the champion had visualized it.

That which he visualized had actualized. But naturally all of this tremendous achievement was not limited to mental practice. Player works. He has always worked, constantly struggling to perfect his stroke, his stance, his entire performance. A few years ago while in his country I wanted to reach Gary Player, who was at home at the time, but missed him on my telephone call. Next morning very early, perhaps at 7:30, from the airport I called again, only to find that he had gone out about an hour earlier, and for what reason? Why, to practice, of course. Always working to improve, always striving to do better, the great Grand Slam golfer had the realistic background upon which to perform the amazing power of visualization.

Also operating in the experience of this great athlete is a power that has worked wonders in his long and outstanding career. "Faith," he says, "is the most dynamic and energizing force in my life . . . faith in God, faith in other people, faith in myself. For me, at least, the three are inseparable." In all the struggles and vicissitudes of intense competition, Gary Player has never lost the inspiration nor the motivation nor the ability—always to keep the positive principle going.

The Relaxed Effort Method

The type of trying that works wonders must also involve the relaxed attitude toward effort when that is indicated. All too many sincere and conscientious people expend every energy in trying hard and even harder to accomplish their goals but finally push their energies to a breaking point without attaining the goals for which they have put forth every ounce of strength. They become victims of the overpress and thus the overstress. The problem under such circumstances is to employ the relaxed trying method; the "easy does it" approach.

This consists of deliberately breaking the strain of constant and undeviating effort, the dogged force of will, the driving persistence, by a letting up; a relaxing of strain. There is a danger in rigid overpressure or insistence upon trying too hard; the creative flow, which is vital to doing anything well and competently, may be subordinated. As a result you just do not work or accomplish efficiently.

I recall one beautiful winter day in the country at our farm on Quaker Hill when I was laboring hard on an article, the deadline for which was looming up in demanding immediacy. Up at the crack of dawn, starting work long before breakfast, I went at this job with the determined attitude that I was going to finish the thing by noontime and get it in the afternoon mail. That was the hard-driving schedule. No deviation from it would be tolerated by me!

"You can do anything if you work and keep on working; if you try and never let up on trying," is what I said to myself as I went to work. All went well for a time and definite progress was being made. The words seemed to march along like soldiers in orderly fashion. There was a rhythmic flow to the ideas, and all in all it seemed to be shaping up as a pretty good piece. "Boy," I exulted, "I'll knock this off in no time flat." But as is often the case, pride goeth before a fall. The inspiration suddenly ran out and to keep it going required redoubled effort. I pumped up my flagging energies but finally had to admit I'd gone stale. The ideas no longer flowed, the words got all messed up. Sentences were laborious and involved and really awkward as well.

Finally I slammed down my pencil, got up, walked around the room, firmly sat down again. "I'll stick this out and see it through. I'll keep at it all day if necessary, but I'm going to finish this job—period," I growled. But it was no go. The inspiration had up and fled, and that which had started out so terrifically had now ground to a stop—an uninspired, dismal stop.

Looking out the window to the snowy landscape, I saw the whited hills silhouetted against a clear blue sky. Tufts of snow clung to the pine trees like cotton balls. Everywhere the snow glistened like myriads of diamonds flung all around by some gigantic hand. It was one of those cold, crystal-clear, perfect winter days. "What," I asked myself sympathetically, "am I doing here cooped up in this house, slaving my life away, when I could be outside there enjoying myself?"

I Fall Into the River

Pushing the papers aside with a masterful "to heck with it," I put on a windbreaker, a fur hat, some warm gloves and went for the kitchen door. There patiently waiting was my huge dog Tonka, all ready for a hike. Tonka and I headed across the lawn on which the snow lay a foot deep; down through a valley and across a meadow, working up a sweat even in 15 degree cold due to the struggle of pushing through deep snow. In the woods dark tree trunks stood stark against the glistening white. Tonka and I stopped to listen to the singing of the wind, which strangely did not seem to interfere with the deep quietness. Tongue hanging out, the dog looked and listened. I, with tongue almost hanging out, did likewise.

Then on we went past the huge old red barn, one of the oldest and largest in Dutchess County, until finally we stood by the little river that splashes down our four-stage waterfall from its source high in the Connecticut hills. Perhaps it was more a creek than a river, actually a "crick," as we called it when I was a boy in Ohio. Anyway, it was full up to the banks and coated over with ice. I watched as Tonka stepped easily across the ice to a place on the far shore where there was a spot of cold water from which he drank with obvious pleasure. I envied him, for the water looked fresh and good, but having read numerous news stories about polluted water, I suffered my thirst.

Tonka, who must weigh close to 150 pounds, seemed to negotiate the ice so well that I decided to follow him across. But I found that there must be a difference between four feet and two, for halfway over the ice broke, depositing me into perhaps three feet of ice-cold water. Struggling back to the bank, I floundered a mile and a half through that heavy snow and uphill all the way, followed by the sympathetic and loyal Tonka. Though the exertion warmed me up, I took the precaution of wrapping myself in a bathrobe before the blazing fireplace, meanwhile swallowing a copious drink of boiling-hot lemonade. "You'll catch your death of cold," warned Ruth, and I had visions of pneumonia putting an end to my "literary" career.

But suddenly like a flash it popped into my head—the idea for which I had been so futilely struggling. Thoughts began to flow out of my mind like that stream into which I had fallen. Rushing back to my study, I put words down on paper so rapidly that the article was finished before lunch, and by four o'clock it was typed, in the post office and on its way.

I do not mean to imply that one can do better, when hard trying doesn't work, by going out and falling into the river, especially when it runs icy cold. But it is a fact that wisdom dictates a backup from overpressure, a detour from excessive effort. Relaxed trying, a combination of effort and tension-breaking, restores an even thought balance and thus allows concepts and expression to flow freely again. In fact, it may have the effect of restoring a person to mental-physical correlation and thereby a recapturing of the effectiveness which intense strain may have stymied.

Drama in a World Series

An old friend was a famous star pitcher a few years back when the Dodgers were in Brooklyn. Carl Erskine made a record for the most strikeouts in World Series play, a record that stood up for a good many years. I often talked with Carl about the relationship of hard trying and the danger of overpressing, as one tended to tense up under pressure. He pointed out the importance of the mental ability to "go away in thought" momentarily into an atmosphere of calm, even while in the midst of a hard-fought game.

He told of one occasion, an extremely hot day when the pressure mounted and he became very tired. While he walked about the pitcher's mound picking up dirt and wiping his hands on his pants, he returned in memory to a misty morning when he and another pitcher were fishing and from across the water came the sound of singing at a morning prayer meeting. The song was an old hymn of peace and quiet. In the few seconds of this "memory trip," Carl recovered strength and poise and performed effectively, with energy to spare.

At another time it was the fifth inning of the fifth game of the World Series and Carl Erskine was on the mound for the Brooklyn Dodgers. That day also happened to be Carl and Betty's fifth wedding anniversary. Carl was going well and had amassed a four-run lead, the score standing at 4-0 in favor of the Dodgers. Perhaps the pitcher was trying too hard and overpressing, the result of which is often to throw him off his rhythm. Whatever the cause, suddenly the opposing team began connecting with the ball and two runs were in with two men on base. Tensed up, Carl threw a fast

127

ball straight over the plate to the next batter, who promptly sent it sailing for a home run. This put the Yankees ahead, 5-4.

In the ensuing bedlam the Brooklyn manager, Charlie Dressen, one of the great managers and a student of human nature, walked slowly from the dugout to the pitcher's mound where Carl waited rather despondently. Dressen took the ball from Carl, tossed it up a couple of times, kicked the dust, then said, surprisingly, "Carl, isn't this your fifth wedding anniversary?" Astonished, Carl replied, "Yes, Mr. Dressen, this is our fifth wedding anniversary."

"Well," continued Dressen, "aren't you going to take Betty out to dinner tonight?"

I think all of us have wondered what is said in those dramatic conferences between pitcher and manager in crisis moments of a baseball game. Carl himself was amazed. He looked around at the great stadium packed with seventy thousand excited fans and here was his manager calmly talking about Carl taking his wife out for a wedding anniversary dinner that night. "Yes, Mr. Dressen, I am taking Betty out for dinner this evening to celebrate five years of marriage."

Dressen handed the ball back to Erskine. "You're my man, Carl. Finish this game before dark." In the six innings that followed of that World Series game, nineteen opposing players came to bat but not one got to first base. The Dodgers drove in two more runs and the game ended in a victory for Erskine by a score of 6-5.

Dressen knew what he was doing. With consummate understanding, faith and psychology, he steadied a pitcher who was trying too hard and therefore pressured. This able manager knew that his pitcher had the ability and the control to win that game if he could relax him. This he did by a simple, human, but extraordinarily adroit method. He employed the simplicities and nostalgia of a loving relationship in such a way as to draw off tension and restore a relaxed and powerful control. He renewed in Carl the power to keep it going under pressure.

Let God Help You Try

I received from one of my readers, Dorothy Sheckels, a beautiful wall hanging done in needlepoint. It is an exquisite piece of work by a woman who had passed through many troubles, including ill health. She was trying always for a better and more useful way of life. After a long period of frustrating circumstances she turned herself over to God saying, "Well, God, if You cannot change me, then just use me as I am."

The idea came to begin doing embroidery for family and friends, and in the process she became quite expert. Then she was asked by someone to do a piece of needlepoint, but her first reaction was that she could not do anything so demanding. But she studied and she tried and tried some more. She had learned to let God help her and accordingly she improved amazingly in this craft. And with it her whole life-style and way of living improved.

I cite this incident, for the piece of needlepoint sent to me expresses a compelling thought of subtle wisdom—don't try to do it all yourself, but let God do it through you. The piece says in needlepoint (and it is beautifully done):

> Trust in the Lord with all
> thine heart and lean not
> unto thine own understanding.
> In all thy ways acknowledge
> Him, and He shall direct thy
> paths.   Prov. 3:5–6

This woman, in circumstances less dramatic than the sports figures previously described and in a setting of ordinary living where most of us are situated, learned a top secret, namely: Don't try too hard; let God help you. When this practice is followed, the result inevitably is unexpected guidance in the form of fresh insights. Edison had a sign on his laboratory wall which read, "There's a better way to do it—find it." That better way is often blocked off by tense and uptight attitudes. The required insights cannot come through. Always in consciousness are ideas that can change your life and greatly improve your performance. The best way I have ever found to start these better ideas flowing is through faith; by letting God who made you now remake you by normalizing your entire personality. Then creative things really start happening.

As one man put it, "I found that I couldn't do it very well, but when I took God into partnership He and I did it very well indeed."

You can do wonders if you will only try and believe and always keep it going.

This chapter has emphasized the following important points:

1. You will never know what great things you can do until you try—really try.
2. Hang in there—stick with it—hammer at it—keep it going.
3. Trying as a continuous process sustained at high level is a viable goal-achiever.
4. Use the amazing power of imagination, the creative technique of imaging, to make the trying more effective.
5. Prayerize, visualize, energize, actualize.
6. Picture your goal; "see" it clearly as now in process of formation, already becoming fact.

7. Practice until you achieve the relaxed trying principle.
8. When trying makes you stale, divert the mind, break the strain. Ideas will start flowing again.
9. Let God help you try. Experts are made by this procedure.
10. Always keep the positive principle going.

EIGHTH
WAY TO KEEP
THE POSITIVE
PRINCIPLE GOING

How to React Creatively to Upsetting Situations

"Everyone has inside himself—what shall I call it—a piece of good news."[1] I noted this striking and thoughtful statement framed and on the wall of a beautiful home in Bermuda. With Commander Geoffrey Kitson, whose home it was, I discussed the meaning of these provocative words. We agreed that each of us does have a big piece of good news deep within ourselves. Such good news is the fact that with God's help we have what it takes to meet all upsetting situations and to react creatively to them.

So, as you read this book, if you are faced with an upsetting situation, the message for you, loud and clear, is that you can handle it, and effectively. And if that upsetting situation has worn you down and perhaps depleted your supply of faith, draw on the positive principle again and this time keep it going. A resupplying of belief in yourself and in God will get you going with increased courage. New insights and a strong grasp on the situation will come, however complex and difficult the situation may appear to be. We use the phrase "may appear," for generally the outcome of any problem, good or otherwise, depends upon how it appears to us. Most outcomes are first determined in mental outlook. So take a strong, positive look at your hitherto upsetting

[1] Sister Mary Corida.

133

situation and apply the positive principle in reacting to it creatively.

First, let us consider a situation which seems to arise periodically, one in which many persons during economic recession or business adjustments may find themselves out of gainful employment. This is a situation which can of course be terribly upsetting. Hardly anyone expressed this problem with more poignancy in the last period of recession than a father of nine children, when he wrote the following newspaper piece:[2]

OUT OF WORK AND SCARED

Let me tell you what it's like for one guy to be 52 years old and jobless.

As a recently fired middle-management executive of a division of one of America's top 500 companies, I have sent out over 150 resumes. Less than 10% have drawn a response of any kind. Five percent drew requests for additional information, while less than four percent resulted in a personal interview. None resulted in a job.

As an infantry veteran of World War II in the South Pacific, I've had some experience with fear, and how men deal with it. I like to feel that I don't scare any easier than the next guy, but to be 52 years old and jobless is to be frightened—frightened to the marrow of your bones. Your days start with it, and end with it. It's all-pervasive. It's numbing. It's mind-boggling.

Things you've always taken for granted fall apart. You can no longer maintain your hospitalization insurance, and for the first time in 28 years you and your family are unprotected against a medical emergency. You are unable to meet the payments on your life insurance. The bank holding your mortgage warns that foreclosure is being considered. Bills to the

[2]Edward B. Furey, Poughkeepsie (N.Y.) *Journal*. Reprinted from *Moneysworth*.

utilities are overdue and you're keeping vital services only through partial payments, aware of the fact that time is running out.

It's to tell a fine 14-year-old son that you haven't got the five bucks you owe him for the great report card he brought home.

It's to pass local merchants on the street and feel embarrassment, wondering when you'll be able to pay them what you owe them.

It's to feel the disintegration of your confidence as a man and your ability to protect your family from economic disaster.

It's to envy just about everybody who has a job, any job.

It's to see the doubt on the faces of your children about what's going on in their house, when so many of their friends are unaffected.

It's to add a crushing dimension to the natural self-doubts that are part of the process of growing older.

It's to stand silently on unemployment lines with other surplus members of America's work force, waiting to sign for your unemployment check.

It's to see what the neighborhood looks like at 10:30 on a Tuesday morning.

It's to feel embarrassed to answer the ring of the telephone at the same hour.

And in the late evening, when your household is quiet and you switch off the bedroom light, it's to be alone, alone like you've never been before. To lie there looking at the darkness and wonder if you're going to lose the home that you've worked all your life for, the home that represents the only equity you've been able to accumulate in 30 years of working and raising a family.

And finally, it's to lie sleepless in bed waiting for the dawn of a new day.

Quite apart from the question of economic conditions that permit such tragedies to occur in our society, our discussion here is limited to the problem of how a person may react creatively in dealing with such an upsetting situation. Perhaps the first step is to remind the individual that he still possesses within himself the "piece of good news," and therefore that there is an answer, that a solution can be found. Accordingly, a basic procedure is to begin and resolutely continue an affirmation that the situation is in no sense hopeless. The affirmation must contain a positive assertion, constantly repeated. Perhaps the following formula may be a guide: "With God's help and guidance I can achieve a creative outcome to this situation, and I am now getting such a solution."

Repeat this affirmation until by a process of intellectual osmosis the idea passes into the unconscious and is accepted as fact. Immediately, then, positive forces will go into operation and produce the actualization of the affirmation. Remember that a negative affirmation is also extremely powerful, and if you should affirm and continue to affirm failure outcomes, the mind will function in a similar manner to actualize a failure pattern.

Therefore the first step is to develop an awareness of your own inherent or built-in creative power; and the second is to affirm positively that successful outcomes not only are possible but are also now operating powerfully and creatively in consciousness, and that they are currently materializing.

Cool It; Don't Panic

A third step in dealing with an upsetting situation is to draw off heat from it and to cool it, calm it and resist panic in any form. So important is this procedure that it might properly rate as step number one. But whether it be point one, two or three, it is absolutely vital never, never, *never* to panic when facing an upsetting situation. I am quite well aware that the avoidance of panic is not easy—far from it. Always the tendency in times of difficulty and crisis is to react emotionally, and the mental cooling process requires strong discipline which is not easily applied when the mind is agitated or alarmed or bitter or angry or in any other way conditioned emotionally.

However, we need at all times to be sensitively aware that the human mind cannot function at its maximum best when it is hot, as overcharged emotion tends to make it. Only when the mind is cool—better still, cold—will it correlate in smooth, well-organized functioning. Only then will it produce those dispassionate, rational and objective insights that lead to solutions. When facing an upsetting situation the objective is to be as collected mentally as possible, for in order to deal with such a situation one must really think, and thinking can be accomplished most effectively only when the emotions are under strict control.

One man who passed through a difficult unemployment experience (and I was reminded of him when I read the newspaper piece printed earlier) told me of a successful formula he used for cooling the mind, for curbing emotion; one that helped immeasurably in maximizing the ability to think and therefore to act constructively. His formula or method was to "pass through the mind" such statements as the following: "Thou wilt keep him in perfect peace, whose mind is stayed on thee."[3] And again: "Come unto me . . . and I will give you rest."[4] And still another: "In quietness and in confidence shall be your strength."[5]

He was quite an ingenious fellow from the standpoint of mental culture in that he could also mentally recon-

[3]Isaiah 26:3.
[4]Matthew 11:28.
[5]Isaiah 30:15.

struct or recall the most quiet and peaceful scenes he had ever experienced. Examples were a covered bridge in Vermont on a colorful autumn day; another, a remote sea beach on the Maine coast where he spent summers in camp as a boy. This practice of "memorized peacefulness," as he described it, seemed to exercise a salutary effect in drawing off heat from his thinking and therefore made him better able to consider pertinent matters objectively and dispassionately. When we are able to think in such balanced manner, we have a much improved chance of capturing creative insights and ideas to help us out of our troubles.

A person who is in panic due to what he regards as a desperate situation is perhaps likely to be impatient with such scientific anti-panic methodology as here described. "You just don't know my situation; you can't really understand," he might declare heatedly. And this reaction is understandable and deserving of sympathy. However, making every allowance, such an attitude can hardly be valid, for many people who have developed the positive principle to support them in upsetting situations do not panic but, on the contrary, act intelligently and in a controlled manner.

Pilot's Arm Cut Off

The horrifying experience of Brian Steed comes to mind.[6] If anyone faced an upsetting situation, it was this Canadian bush pilot who operated a light pontoon plane in isolated areas. A company had sent him to scout a wilderness lake as a possible supply base. He had landed on the lake with no difficulty, but when he headed into the wind for takeoff his cap was blown into the water. It was a favorite hat and he did not want to

---

[6]Retold from a story in *Guideposts*.

lose it, so he turned the plane near to the floating cap and throttled to low speed. Climbing down to the pontoon to grab the cap, which was bobbing in the water, a slight pitch caught him off balance. His feet slipped and he plunged forward toward the propeller.

Brian Steed felt a whack on the shoulder and then found himself thrashing in the water. He did not feel hurt particularly and concluded that probably he had hit a strut. But his right arm did not feel quite right, and he swam with his left. Then in attempting to climb back into the plane he discovered to his horror that the right arm had been completely severed by the turning propeller and that he was bleeding profusely at the shoulder. At once he knew that unless something could be done quickly he would certainly bleed to death. Then came the thought that perhaps death was to be desired, for how could he live without a right arm? But this thought passed quickly as he remembered his wife and small children. He was definitely growing fainter, blood streaming from the shoulder stump. Here was, indeed, a setup for panic—right arm cut off, severe bleeding, alone in a wilderness and far from help.

Why was there no panic in this crisis? The answer! This bush pilot was a man of powerful faith—the real thing. He knew where a better-than-human help was to be found. He found strength to climb into the cockpit. This Helper showed him how to apply, with one hand, a makeshift tourniquet to stanch the flow of blood from the shoulder. He gunned the plane to take off, flying without any tendency toward fainting to a base camp where he received help from two friends who flew him to a hospital for treatment.

Says pilot Brian Steed of his incredible experience, which could have been completely shattering, "Many people have told me that most bush pilots would have panicked had they found themselves in my predicament. Perhaps I would have, too, had I not known that there is truth in those words, 'God is our refuge and strength, a very present help in trouble.' "[7] Obviously that Help was very much present when his trouble struck. Anyone can panic, but people with the quality of faith which this bush pilot possessed are able to handle panic and therefore deal creatively with upsetting situations, no matter how terrifying they may be.

He Solved an Unemployment Problem

In thinking of the fifty-two-year-old man whose heart-moving article is included earlier in this chapter, I recall a similar case from years ago. This chapter is being written at the Mountain View House in the White Mountains, a beautiful hotel where our longtime friend Schuyler Dodge is the owner and to which our family has been coming for many years. It looks out on the spectacular Presidential Range in New Hampshire. Here, some twenty years ago, I received a long-distance telephone call from a very distracted man. It was shortly after *The Power of Positive Thinking* was published, and this man, having just read the book, was strongly impelled to talk with me. I had never met him and so, of course, knew nothing about him.

As I listened to the story of a lost job and futile efforts to find a new position with no result, it occurred to me that perhaps by allowing him to talk out the problem he might possibly develop his own solution, as often happens. This man had the greatly-to-be-desired ability to state a problem in organized fashion, which of course indicated an exact quality of mind. He was not in any sense negative or complaining or bitter, though under-

[7]Psalm 46:1.

standably he seemed disturbed that he had been unable to make a business connection, particularly since his savings were practically exhausted. The sense of anxiety came through in his conversation, but it was controlled, though obviously not without effort.

Finally I said, "Look, you don't know the answer to your problem and neither do I. So I suggest that we bring in a Consultant, One whose know-how is of top quality, and put the matter directly to Him. Then let's leave it to Him to point the way."

He at once grasped the meaning of this suggestion and said, "Okay, you talk to Him for both of us."

So then and there over the telephone, separated from my caller by a thousand miles or more, I sent out a request asking for the needed guidance. On the supposition that somewhere there was a job for this man, I asked that the man and the job be brought together. "Let me know what happens," I said, and was rather surprised at the reply: "I've got a strange but strong feeling that something is going to happen, and soon. Thanks a lot."

Then the positive principle went to work to produce an intelligent result.

Perhaps three weeks later I received a phone call from this man at my New York office. It seems that he had secured a position with a restaurant, a totally different type of occupation from any he had contemplated. This job did not pay nearly so much as his former connection, but enough to get by on. And he must have done all right in this new business, for later on he acquired two restaurants of his own which he operated successfully until his death some seventeen years later.

When asked how the job opportunity had come about, he replied, "Funny thing. It was really weird. You see, I was eating in this restaurant and idly got to thinking that it seemed a well-managed place. It was on the inexpensive side but everything was neat and clean and obviously it was operated by someone with imagination. Suddenly I had a strong feeling that I would like to work for these people." He hesitated. "It was almost like being home, as if, you might say, I was meant to be there. So while paying my check I asked if I might speak with the manager.

"He was a friendly fellow and I became aware that he was sizing me up. It was more than a perfunctory conversation. Finally he said, 'Well, it's sort of funny, but maybe you have happened along at the right time. You see, I've just lost my right-hand man, who died ten days ago. Been trying since to handle everything myself. But I'm lost without Ralph, as he seemed to know just what to do all the time, always on top of things. Know anything about this business?' he asked.

"I just had to level with him. 'Not a thing except general business principles,' I said. 'But your restaurant seems to have—what shall I call it—a spirit. It's different and imaginative. I suppose the way to run a restaurant is to give people good food in a pleasant atmosphere at reasonable prices and make a reasonable profit on your investment.'

"The owner grinned at that. 'Not bad, not bad at all.' Then he continued, 'I have been expecting the right man to come along. [Much later when they had become friends he confessed he had prayed for that "right man."] Well, give me some references. Are you willing to take the long hours this business requires?'

"I'll stick with you all the way," my man replied, and added, "I sort of feel that this job was meant to be." And indeed so it proved, for later he became a partner, then, on the other man's retirement, bought him out and ultimately added a second restaurant. His explanation of the entire experience was succinct and to him represented the facts. "Someone," he said, "was on my side." And we may add Someone is always on your side, too. Never doubt it.

The In-and-With-It People

These persons who react creatively to upsetting experiences invariably demonstrate certain impressive qualities. They do not panic; they do not emotionalize. They think cooly, dispassionately, objectively. This type of person takes a positive viewpoint, rejecting the negatives no matter how unpropitious the situation may appear to be. And without exception they have a sustaining faith that helps to keep them going as they keep the positive principle activated.

This is the twenty-fourth book I have written, and in each book I have strongly stressed spiritual faith as a necessary factor in successful living. But now and then someone will write or say something to the effect that "I take your practical suggestions, but skip the religious stuff." Such objections are a minuscule minority in this better-educated era, but there are still a few who seem to have the notion that spiritual techniques are somehow a kind of aberration to be differentiated from practicality.

In their old-fashioned view, the practitioners of religious truth principles have a sort of "oddball" streak. On the contrary, the in-and-with-it people regard spiritual concepts as a truly scientific way of life. Science, of course, is a thought pattern based on demonstrable techniques. Science in the field of thought is no less valid than science in a laboratory, for in both instances it is based on workable and proven formulas.

Indeed, the prophecy made years ago by one of America's greatest geniuses of science is currently being verified to such an extent that knowledgeable persons now recognize the validity of spiritual principles as verifiable scientific procedure. These principles work when worked. Faith produces results. Power operates through the mind as surely as through wires. Communication comes directly into consciousness no less surely than television pictures are transmitted via satellite.

The above-mentioned scientist was the famed Dr. Charles Steinmetz, who, when asked what line of research would have the greatest development during the next fifty years, said:

> I think the greatest discoveries will be made along spiritual lines. Some day people will learn that material things do not bring happiness and are of little use in making men and women creative and powerful. Then the scientists of the world will turn their laboratories over to the study of God and prayer and the spiritual forces which, as yet, have been hardly scratched. When that day comes, the world will see more advancement in one generation than it has seen in the last four.[8]

I Have Had Upsetting Situations, Too

In discussing reaction to upsetting situations and how to keep going under difficult and trying circumstances, I am not here dealing with a theoretical matter, for I also have had my share of such problems. One arose after *The Power of Positive Thinking* became what in the book trade they call, rather exaggeratedly I always thought, a "runaway best-seller." The book did have and has continued to have an enormous sale. For some reason this roused the ire of some of the left-wingish and far-out liberal clergy. Indeed, their violently hostile attitude was described by one magazine as "the rage of the intellectuals." At any rate, they had it in for me and berated me

[8]Reader's Digest.

behind and before, even to the extent of preaching sermons against what they angrily called "Pealism."

Prior to this experience I had always believed that all ministers were uniformly gentlemanly persons who, while they might disagree with one's ideas and strongly express divergent opinion, still did not attack an individual as a person or use harsh and intemperate language in castigating him. And I hasten to add that the vast majority of the clergy are kindly and considerate people who, if they take a different viewpoint, do so with courtesy. But in the violent and bitter-tongued few I found what literally amounted to an appalling hate psychosis which seemed shocking indeed.

Why Were They So Het Up?

The rationale for this violent anti reaction was, one supposes, that the book was written in a direct and simple style using language and thought forms readily understandable by the average man on the street. Indeed, the book was intended for him and not for supersophisticated scholars, although perhaps any person might have used its principles to advantage.

Since the point of view of the book was that through positive attitudes one could achieve better things in life and do a more constructive job on oneself, the critics, who sometimes seem constitutionally negative, bristled at the mere mention of the word "success," even when it was not intended to mean making a pile of money or getting one's name in the paper. Since, if things should go better both for individuals and for society there would be less to carp about, the negativist tends to take a jaundiced view of the concept of positive thinking. And finally, the book being highly successful from a publishing viewpoint in terms of the number of copies sold, that pesky jealous element when a colleague is fortunate enough to have a project turn out well can sometimes affect attitudes, rationalize it as we will.

Well, whatever the reasons, and perhaps some criticism was well founded, the barrage of opposition let loose on me was formidable. I was belabored hot and heavy by my vocal and vindictive detractors. The situation was potentially upsetting indeed. As a matter of fact, I was bewildered and somewhat hurt and hard put to it to understand this mistreatment, for my simple book was intended only to help people. Of course, thousands of kindly persons came to my support and I felt upheld and strengthened by their confidence. But still, nobody can be attacked, often viciously, as I was, especially by men in one's own line or profession, and not tend to be upset.

I Found the Way
to Overcome the Situation

The natural tendency in such a situation is to fight back, to give as good as received. Some friends suggested, "Tell them off in words they cannot fail to understand." But this did not seem advisable, and besides, it would constitute a denial of the truth principles I believed and taught. Accordingly, not without some personal struggle, I decided upon the policy of putting into active practice the principles of scientific truth which I had suggested as viable to others in upsetting situations.

1. I decided not to answer criticism or to make any explanation, nor to defend myself, but to take it in silence.
2. I decided to examine every criticism to ascertain whether it was valid, and if so, to try to correct my own position. For example, once in Chicago I was met by reporters who showed me a violent attack on me by the then Dean of the Yale School of

Theology. One reporter read it to me and asked for a comment. I said, "The Dean is a distinguished man, and if he feels about me as he stated, then it is my duty to re-examine myself and my teachings." Being all set for fuel to keep the fire burning, they were obviously disappointed. No story in that, from their reportorial point of view.

3. I went out of my way to be nice to my enemies. From time to time I issued a list of recommended books and gave highest marks to a book by one of my chief detractors. This was done only because I considered it an excellent piece of work. The book was considered on an objective and not an emotional basis.

4. I continued quietly to teach that Christianity is a scientific, practical, workable way of life; a philosophy of thought and action that can help anyone in whatever circumstance. Everyday people by the thousands accepted that teaching to their great benefit, as reported in a mass of letters of appreciation.

Well, either I outlived my enemies or they came to see things in a different light or the viewpoints I expressed gained wider acceptance. Whatever happened, the opposition finally subsided. And many who once opposed me violently wrote that they had changed their minds, not only about my ideas but about me personally. I did not necessarily want or even expect people to admit that they were wrong and that I was right. What I really wanted was to demonstrate to myself and perhaps to others that spiritual truth principles are viable and will work when truly worked. It was my desire to prove conclusively, to my own satisfaction primarily, that I could react creatively to an upsetting situation. And I found that indeed I could, with God's help, keep the positive principle operative. Enthusiasm for the message I was dedicated to communicate was not one whit diminished.

When Grief Comes

It so happens that, because my writings deal primarily with people-centered problems of a very personal nature, thousands of letters are received from individuals everywhere telling of upsetting situations which they face. To sit down with, say, a hundred such letters is profoundly moving and can be even a heartrending experience, for such letters reveal the wide panorama of human suffering. Every Good Friday, for example, our Foundation for Christian Living conducts a twenty-four-hour Prayer Vigil dealing with from 25,000 to 40,000 requests for prayers which come in for that day. If you wished to know what is disturbing or upsetting people, a sampling of these communications would awe you by the extent and depth of suffering and anxiety which are daily prevalent everywhere. Looking at a crowd of people in a church or music hall or theater or at an athletic event, one observes no evidence of such problems. It is the mark of a sophisticated person to dissemble, not to reveal outwardly, the inner fears and troubles which afflict him. But to one whose work it is to deal with such matters in a sympathetic manner, the full extent of burdens is poured out without reserve.[9]

One of the most acute of all upsetting situations is that of grief occasioned by the death of someone dearly loved. Scarcely any form of mental pain quite equals this poignant human experience. It is a blow, a shock, a devastation that cuts deeply and acutely into the bereaved person's mind. This experience, inevitable in due course to everyone, must be faced, when it comes, with dignity, strength and understanding. But this of course is not easy to do. Indeed, it is an upsetting situa-

[9]If I can be helpful to any reader, please write me c/o Foundation for Christian Living, Pawling, N.Y. 12564.

tion from which recovery and healing of mind can be an extraordinarily difficult process.

To be supportive of a person suffering from the shock of grief, a genuine transference of love is no doubt a most effective form of helpfulness. But many persons admit feeling inadequate to expressing the concern and sympathy really felt under such painful circumstances. Actually, words are not vitally important; the conveyance by attitude of the felt affection performs its own healing.

As a very young man I was called upon to conduct the funeral of a little girl in Brooklyn, New York. It was only the second funeral of my then brief career as a minister, and the first for a child. The body of the sweet little girl lay in a white casket. I remember that she was dressed in white and had pink ribbons in her golden hair. It really broke me up. I stood hesitantly, trying to say something to comfort the crushed young parents, but the words would not come. Finally I went across the room to the parents, the mother only twenty-one and the father twenty-three, impulsively put my arms around them and said brokenly, "Listen, Jim and Helen—listen and never forget it—God loves you." That was all I could say. Some forty years later the father told me, "When you put your arms around us that terrible day, we knew that you loved us and," he added, "you made us know, really know, that the love of God is real. And I've loved Him—and you—ever since." The love that passed between us that day taught these sad and crushed parents how to keep going in the traumatic pain of grief.

Love, the Great Healer

Fine words, facility of speech, sound argument, even convincing expressions of faith—none of these has the power to convey warmth as does the outgoing of genuine and loving friendship. Indeed, I have often felt that the power of the words of Scripture to comfort the sorrowing is largely due to the fact that they give assurance of God's love. For that reason they never fail to provide comfort and serenity. How many countless thousands, in the upsetting situation of sorrow and loneliness, have found peace and solace in such grief-healing words as "I am the resurrection, and the life: he that believeth in me, though he were dead, yet shall he live: And whosoever liveth and believeth in me shall never die."[10] Or, again: "In my Father's house are many mansions: . . . I go to prepare a place for you. . . . that where I am, there ye may be also."[11] And the incomparable picture of a loving Father: "They shall hunger no more, neither thirst any more; neither shall the sun light on them, nor any heat. For the Lamb which is in the midst of the throne shall feed them, and shall lead them unto living fountains of waters: and God shall wipe away all tears from their eyes."[12]

A leader of industry, onetime president of General Motors Corporation, lost his wife after more than fifty years of marriage. Shortly thereafter mutual friends indicated that Alfred P. Sloan wished to talk with me, as he was inconsolable. He fixed his penetrating eyes on me and with characteristic directness said, "I want to ask a straight question and want a straight answer. No vague generalization or weasel speculation."

"Okay," I said, "you ask the question and you'll get a straight answer."

"What I want to know is this: Will I ever be with my wife again or is she forever lost to me?"

"If you live in faith as she did, you will meet her in the

[10]John 11:25-26.
[11]John 14:2-3.
[12]Revelation 7:16-17.

afterlife where there is no separation. And meanwhile you will sense her nearness even on this earth."

He looked searchingly into my eyes. "How sure are you?" he insisted.

"Absolutely sure," I replied. He was too big a mentality to demand philosophical proofs. All that he wanted was a positive principle on which to rest his own momentarily shaky faith. He then went on to tell me how much he depended upon his wife; how, even in business decisions, he trusted her judgment. Touchingly, one became aware how even a strong man, seemingly self-sufficient, had a sense of dependence upon his companion of the years. As I sat looking at this big, intelligent but wounded and lonely man, I felt a surge of love for him. But you can hardly tell a tough man like this that you loved him, so without thinking I walked over and gently laid my hand on his head. He looked up like a child with tears in his eyes. As he showed me to the door and bade me good-bye with a crushing handclasp, all he said was, "Thanks. I'm okay now. I can keep going."

I'll Never Forget Myron Robinson

I have personal reason to know how love without words can help overcome the upsetting feelings caused by grief because I knew Colonel Myron Robinson. He was a big, rough kind of man, a prominent New Jersey politician in his day. He had a heart as big as all outdoors. And he was a member of my church in New York.

One Friday night some years ago after a memorable evening with my mother and the entire family, I took a night train from upstate New York to New York City, as I had a speaking engagement in a church at Elberon on the Jersey coast on the coming Sunday morning.

But early Saturday morning, shortly after arrival in the city, I had a telephone call from my wife, Ruth, that my mother had just died of a thrombosis. Shocked and grieved, I told Ruth that I would return immediately to Canisteo, New York, the family home, but in talking it over we decided that Mother would want me to carry on and keep my engagement to preach the Gospel, in which she believed so deeply. But I was sad and sorrowful and under shock. It was so unbelievable. My mother, whom I adored, was dead.

On Sunday morning early I boarded a train at Penn Station and sat disconsolately looking out the window when along came Myron Robinson walking through the coach. He took the seat beside me. "Where are you going, Myron?" I asked.

"To a big Republican clambake down at Ocean City. Big time today. Everyone will be there. Wouldn't miss it."

"Well, I hope you have a good time," I remarked.

Suddenly he looked at me. "What's the trouble, Norman? You're not your usual self. Something bothering you?"

So I told him what had happened in not too many words, as it sort of broke me up to talk about it. All Myron did was to pat me on the knee with his big hand.

When we came to my station of Elberon, to my surprise Myron left the train also. "Why are you getting off here? You have to stay on for Ocean City."

"Oh, I've decided I want to go to church with you instead of that clambake. Don't really like 'em, anyway," he said evasively. He accompanied me to church, sat right in front of me in the first pew, and took me to lunch following. We returned to the station and boarded the train back to New York with hardly any conversation between us. Arriving in Penn Station, where he was going uptown and I downtown, he stopped a moment and a look, really a beautiful look, came upon his face. He punched me in the chest. "I understand, boy, I understand. You've helped me through some hard ones; hope I've been a little help today." Whereupon to hide tears he turned with a wave of the hand and was gone.

Well, Myron Robinson has now himself gone over to the other side, but I will never forget this kindly man who had a heart full of love, a lot of which spilled over to me on that sad day long ago. He helped me to react creatively to one of my most upsetting situations and to keep going on the basis of the positive principle.

In this chapter on the important matter of reacting creatively to upsetting situations, the following points have been made:

1. Everyone has inside himself a piece of good news.
2. Affirm daily, "With God's help and guidance I am now getting creative outcomes to upsetting situations."
3. In tough situations, never panic, always cool it.
4. Remember, there is always Someone on your side.
5. Never make judgments emotionally. Think dispassionately and objectively.
6. Never react emotionally to criticism to the extent of allowing it to affect sound judgment. Analyze yourself to determine whether it is justified. If it is, correct yourself. Otherwise, go on about your business.
7. Always affirm there is an answer and solution to any problem and that you can find it; indeed, that you are now finding that answer.
8. When grief comes, remember and never forget that God loves you. He will see you through, always and surely.

NINTH
WAY TO KEEP
THE POSITIVE
PRINCIPLE GOING

You Can Cope With Anything; You Really Can

You can cope with anything; you really can. And one thing is sure—the only way to handle this life successfully is to learn to cope. *Cope* means to handle, to confront, to stand up to, to deal with.

Two Little Girls

And finding out that one must cope is often encountered early in life. It is only as one develops this skill that ultimate and final personal victory comes. I happened to be on a Florida-bound train one day, but my destination was the Thirtieth Street station in Philadelphia. At North Philadelphia two little girls boarded the train. They were about ten and twelve years of age, I judged. I saw them first outside the window saying a tearful good-bye to two middle-aged people.

There was an empty seat alongside of me and the older girl sat there; the other little girl took the seat across the aisle. They were very sweet, demure, well dressed; indeed, very ladylike. They were wearing little immaculate white gloves. The girl sitting next to me was quite solemn; and then I saw a tear, like a pearl, on her cheek. In her little hands she clutched a camera. So I asked, "Are you going to take some pictures?"

She replied in a tone so low that I could hardly hear.

"We love them so, and we have to leave them. We love them so very much."

"Whom are you leaving, your parents?"

"No, our grandparents."

"And where are you going?" I asked.

"To St. Petersburg, to see our father, to live with him. We haven't seen him for three years. We hardly know him. [Apparently a broken family situation.] But our grandparents—we don't want to leave them. We love them so much."

"Oh," I said, "you'll like St. Petersburg, with its blue sparkling water, its golden sunlight, its white beaches, its fine people. And your father will be so glad to have his little girls. Just go down there and love him."

She was silent. Finally she said, as though speaking to herself, "But God will take care of us." By this time we had arrived at Thirtieth Street station in Philadelphia and I arose to leave. She stood up. Very politely and gravely she extended her hand to me, a stranger.

"Yes, honey," I said, "never forget it; God will take care of you." As the long sleek train pulled out of the station heading south, I reflected on the little human drama just experienced. Two frightened, lonely little girls, going out into the unknown, were learning early in life that it is necessary to cope. But they had also learned a basic philosophy: With God's help you can cope with anything—you can, for sure.

Of course, when we say that you can cope with anything, it is making an almost incredible claim. But, you see, we have an incredible God to support us. He is more than equal to any crisis, any difficulty in this world. We are told: "With God nothing shall be impossible."[1] It doesn't say that with God some things

[1]Luke 1:37.

156

are not impossible. It says that "nothing" shall be impossible. Again in the Scriptures: "Eye hath not seen, nor ear heard, neither have entered into the heart of man, the things which God hath prepared for them that love him."[2] And one of those tremendous things is the ability to cope with whatever difficulty, frustration or fear may assail us. Another statement gives assurance: "I can do all things through Christ which strengtheneth me."[3]

It is never very smart to disclaim the possibility of a great, even incredible attainment. Theodore N. Vail, a prominent industralist, said, "Real difficulties can be overcome; it is only the imaginary ones that are unconquerable." Right, mostly; but even the imaginary ones can be overcome by right thinking. No difficulty, real or imaginary, is impregnable. But in asserting the claim that you can cope with anything, I remind you of a subtle and sound comment by the writer William Feather: "Success is seldom achieved by people who contemplate the possibility of failure." So hold the thought, hold it tenaciously, that you can cope with anything, especially when you allow God to help you.

Grab a Thistle

And how is this incredible feat accomplished? First of all, never vaguely and indecisively fool around with a difficulty; take hold of it and handle it. Do not be afraid, timorous or doubtful. Simply grab hold of the problem and deal with it masterfully.

In the office of John Bowles, a businessman, I learned of a number of difficulties he had overcome. I thought he seemed very relaxed and unhurt. So I said, "John, how come you were able to handle all you have been

[2]I Corinthians 2:9.
[3]Philippians 4:13.

telling me about? These troubles would be sufficient to overwhelm many people."

He pointed to a vase in which was a big thistle. "Why a thistle?" I asked. "Couldn't you get a more exotic flower?"

"Oh," he replied, "since I experienced all those difficulties the thistle represents qualities most people do not recognize."

"There must be something behind that remark," I vouchsafed.

"There certainly is. Tell you what, take hold of that thistle," he directed.

"I don't like the looks of it; it's spiny; it will sting and hurt."

"Go ahead," he urged, "take hold of it."

Hesitatingly I reached out and gingerly touched it. "It pricks," I complained.

"You must be more of a philosopher than that," he said. "You see, the thistle represents the difficulties of life. And if you know how to handle a thistle, you have learned a primary step in handling difficulties. So grab that whole thistle; grab it hard." I did and, believe it or not, it didn't hurt a bit. It crushed in my hand.

Of course, this incident does not mean that difficulties, when you stand up to them, won't hurt. But they will hurt far less if you handle them forthrightly. When you have a difficulty with which you must cope, don't hold off; grab it, deal with it.

She Takes Life in Her Two Hands

It's like the lady I met in a radio broadcasting studio. She was interviewing several of us, and the conversation turned to some rather deep subjects. I had noticed, as she walked into the broadcasting room, that she was crippled, with one leg shorter than the other. And she was no glamour girl either, being along in years. But she had a beautiful face; actually there was a kind of light on it.

On the show we got to talking about human difficulty, and she said, "Really, there is only one way to handle difficulty. Simply trust God and believe He is with you and helping you all the time. Using that principle, I simply take hold of life with my two hands and handle whatever comes."

I glanced at her hands, noting that they were very small, even delicate, and I thought, "There is not much strength in those hands, but there is a lot of power in the woman." Aloud I said, "Your hands are little, but you tell me that you take hold of life with those two hands."

"Oh," she said, "I also have a secret. I know that my hands are small, but if I put my little hands in the two great big hands of God, that makes four hands. And with God, remember, nothing is impossible."

So, when something very tough comes along with which you must cope, the best procedure is simply to deal with it forthrightly and at once. Handle your difficulty by visualizing your two hands as being placed in the hands of God. This "four hand" concept means that nothing is impossible. Remember this dynamic radio personality. She made a lasting impression on me because of her keen insight into the problem of coping. She underscored the fact that you can cope with anything if you simply grab hold of the matter strongly and intelligently and keep the positive principle going.

So, when you have a big difficulty, the number-one technique is to say to yourself: "With God nothing is impossible." Say that affirmatively and always with faith. Continue that affirmation. Then relax, get quiet physically and mentally, cool it, and believe that the necessary power is coming through to help you handle the situation. In this manner you will learn to keep the power to cope always operative. At all times be philosophical, be relaxed and quietly thoughtful. Do this and the coping process will become easier and surer.

I Find an Old Diary

At our farmhouse in the country my wife recently got on a housecleaning "binge." She insisted that we needed to discard some things, and she started with a closet. It is astonishing how much stuff can accumulate in a closet, and this was a big one. Away back in that closet I found a box in which was a diary written by my father. It began in the spring of the year 1888.

Father went to school when they taught real penmanship, and his handwriting was beautiful. The ink was good, too, for it was very clear after all these years. It was a moving experience to read this diary of my father, who meant so much to me. It stated that he was valedictorian of his high school class. In fact, the diary began with commencement night, which, strangely enough, was in the middle of April in 1888. They had to get through school before spring planting, presumably. There were six students in the class, four boys and two girls. He named them, and I remembered every one from my own youth. The diary told quite a lot about the young boy who later became my father. Let me record a few of his entries:

> Thursday, May 31, 1888
>> I shovelled gravel today. I get $1.25 per day.
>> Went to Young Folks prayer meeting tonight.
> Wednesday, June 6, 1888
>> At the Democrat Convention in St. Louis Grover Cleveland was renominated for President of the United States.
>> I went to Young Folks prayer meeting tonight.

160

I went swimming for the first time this year.
Thursday, June 7, 1888
     Allen G. Thurman was nominated for Vice
     President of the United States.
     I went to missionary meeting at Dr. Garner's
     tonight.
     Went swimming.
Wednesday, June 25, 1888
     Gen. Benjamin Harrison was nominated for
     President by the Republican Party today. Also
     Morton of New York for Vice President.
     I took my last chew of tobacco today. I also smoked
     my last cigar. I mean by this that I quit.

I never knew that he chewed or even smoked. But it
indicates that away back there he was coping with a habit
that bothered him. But he learned how to cope; he went
to the young people's prayer meeting and the mission-
ary meeting, and so was developing a coping faith.

That fall he entered the Medical College of Ohio, as it
was called at that time. He studied hard and became a
physician. Later he became a preacher, for he could not
resist the "call." But he was always a physician type of
preacher, dealing with health of body, mind and soul.

The diary goes on to enumerate something else with
which he had to cope—he didn't have much money. His
father, Samuel Peale, ran a general store in the little
town of Lynchburg, Ohio, where they lived, and from
him he learned to be careful with the little money he
had. He kept an accurate account of all he spent. Note
the price structure of that time:

September 10, 1888 (At College)

Board one week	$2.00
Room rent one week	1.25
Shave	.10
Oyster stew	.20
1 dozen bananas	.05

Dinner	.15
Supper	.10
Postage stamp	.02
Candy for brother	.05
One load of coal	2.00
Church collection	.05
Gave to a poor woman	.10

Those figures indicate how matters stood financially in this country in those days. The average person was not affluent; but there is every indication that he was strong and sturdy, with a deep faith that helped in everyday living.

Toward the end of the diary my father expressed the coping wisdom he had learned, the positive principle he had mastered:

> As a young boy and in my later experiences I discovered a great truth, and it is this: If you stay close to Jesus and have faith in Him, He will see you through anything. He always has and He always will.

My dear father wrote those words on September 10, 1888, when he was eighteen years old. He never knew that one of his sons would be quoting them in a book a long lifetime later. But the principles that my father found workable so many years ago helped him to cope in his day. They are still workable currently. So, as my father put it, "Stay close to Jesus." Always believe that with God, nothing is impossible. By these sound principles you can cope with anything, you really can.

One thing is sure: We are all going to face difficulties in this life. Indeed, there will be lots of them, and some are bound to be severe and acute, even painful. What we do about these difficulties will determine whether circumstances master us or whether we master circumstances. Marcus Aurelius, the great Roman philosopher, is credited with a picturesque statement, one that is surely packed with truth: "Man must be arched and buttressed from within, else the temple wavers to the dust."

In coping with your difficulties, it is of vital importance to develop a philosophical attitude. Do not become tense; never get worked up; always remain unperturbed. Remember, easy does it. Never let yourself be disturbed. Be philosophical. Always maintain emotional balance. Keep the mind operating and in constant control of the emotions.

Visit to a Shinto Shrine

Once in Tokyo I was visiting a Shinto shrine. It is approached down a long avenue of small shops or stalls. In the center of the plaza fronting the temple stands a huge Japanese-style urn from which steaming incense emanates. Tradition has it that if you have an illness or any bodily weakness and you direct the incense over the affected part, you will be healed. I noticed that people were using a circular motion with hands and arms to direct the incense toward various portions of the body. One man, whom I immediately took to be an American, was waving the incense in the direction of his heart. A look of unquestioning faith showed on his face.

"Do you think this incense will heal you?" I asked.

"Why not?" he replied. "They say it will."

"Continue to believe it," I answered. "But how come you are directing the incense toward your heart?"

"Because that is the weakest place in my body."

So after he stepped aside, I waved the steam onto my head.

Believe me, the head *is* most important; for when you face a difficulty it is so terribly necessary always to keep the mind calm and quiet in order that it may be controlled and thereby function efficiently. Of course, that will not always be easy to accomplish. But in order to cope with your difficulties it is important to cultivate the qualities of a philosopher. Be quiet and thoughtful, take things as they come. And always depend upon the calm knowledge that you can be master of anything that may happen to you.

Philosophical Baseball Player

When the Brooklyn Dodgers National League baseball club was in Brooklyn playing in the old Ebbets Field, I knew almost every man on the Dodger roster. One player was a powerful hitter, averaging regularly over .300, which is good and then some.

One night he was coming to our house for dinner with some of his teammates. It had not been possible for me to go to the game that day in early April, but I did listen to part of the game on the radio as I drove in my car to and from engagements.

This mighty hitter came to bat in the second inning and ignominiously struck out—one, two three. I turned off the radio.

That night when the players came to the house this hitter, to my surprise, was in a happy and relaxed mood. "I was sorry to hear that you struck out in the second inning today," I said.

"Oh," he replied, "that isn't all of it. I struck out again in the fourth inning."

Astonished, I asked, "Do you mean to tell me that you can be so unconcerned about striking out twice in one of the early games of the season?"

"Why not?" he replied. "You see, on the basis of my batting average I will strike out about ninety times in the season, and I'm always comforted by the law of averages." I thought that was quite a mouthful for a baseball player. "Yes," he continued, "that law of averages is a great comfort. So today when the game was over and I went into the clubhouse, I said to the boys, 'What do you know! Isn't it great? I only have eighty-eight more times to strike out this season!' "

That is what you can reasonably call a relaxed, philosophical attitude toward a difficulty.

Most difficulties are handled effectively in proportion to the degree to which we untense ourselves. Though this fact was pointed out in the previous chapter, I must underscore it here, for calmness of mind is vital to coping with problems. An uptight, nervous individual is not likely to get into the easy flow of personality in which the thinking process can grapple with difficulty efficiently; when troubled with panic and apprehension feelings, such a mind cannot function with the cool, philosophical attitude of the batter who took comfort in the law of averages.

Nine Guidelines for Coping

Some years ago I worked out nine effective guidelines for coping with difficulties which have been personally helpful, and these include the positive principle we have been discussing:

1. Don't panic. Keep calm. Use your head. Think.
2. Never be overwhelmed. Never dramatize the difficulty. Affirm confidently, "God and I can handle it."
3. Practice "de-confusion." To do so, write on paper every element of the difficulty, mentally clarifying each part.
4. Skip the postmortems. Take the problem from where you are at this instant.

5. Look for an answer, not for the whole problem, but for the next step.
6. Practice creative listening. Get quiet so that insights can come through your mind.
7. Always ask what is the right thing to do, for nothing wrong ever turns out right.
8. Keep thinking, keep believing, keep working, keep praying.
9. Keep on actively employing the positive principle.

Those are nine workable guidelines. Practice them diligently and you can develop the ability to cope with your difficulties in an effective and certain manner. I suggest that they be written on a card small enough to fit into your pocket. Read them every day until they become a definite part of your mental equipment.

Help Others Cope and You Help Yourself

Another workable and effective way to meet and overcome difficulties is to take on someone else's problems. It is a strange fact, but you can often handle two difficulties—your own and somebody else's—better than you can handle your own alone. That truth is based on a subtle law of self-giving or outgoingness whereby you develop a self-strengthening in the process. If you have a tough difficulty, look around until you find somebody who has a worse difficulty than yours, then start helping that individual. You will find in so doing that your own problem, when finally you have helped the other person with his, will be much simpler, much clearer, much easier to handle.

I often think of a story told by Arthur Gordon about the editor of a small-town weekly newspaper, a man who was having some difficult problems. One day the editor's neighbor, a man named Bill, took his wife and little son out on the river in a canoe. Suddenly the canoe overturned. Both wife and husband were good swimmers. They tried desperately to save their boy, but tragically he was swept away and drowned. The father was inconsolable. "Why did I do this?" he berated himself. "Why didn't I do that?" So he argued in futility and desperation. Ceaselessly he walked the streets. People would see him on country roads, walking, walking, always walking.

One night Jack, the newspaper editor, was working late in his office. About midnight came a rap on his door and there, disconsolate, stood his neighbor, Bill. "You're out late tonight, Bill. What are you doing?"

"I'm just walking, Jack, just walking. You see, I can't forget. Why did that have to happen? Why did I take the boy out in the canoe? Why couldn't I rescue him? I can't understand it, Jack."

"Come in, Bill. Sit down and let's talk." Bill slumped in the chair. "I can't talk. I just don't feel like talking."

"Okay," the editor said, "that's all right. Just sit there and I'll go on with my work. Whenever you're ready to talk, let me know." After a while he asked, "Bill, how about a cup of coffee? It will warm you up."

Bill said, "Yes, I'd be glad to have one. But I'm still not ready to talk."

It got to be on toward two o'clock in the morning. Then Bill said, "Now, Jack, I'm ready to talk." For an hour he reasoned it all out, lived it all over again. Jack listened. There are times when one of the most helpful things a person can do for another is simply to listen and let that individual know that you care. This was one of those times. Finally, completely spent, Bill slowed to a stop. "I guess that's all I've got to say tonight, Jack." He got up to go.

Jack put his hand on the broken man's shoulder. "We all love you," he said kindly. "I wish I could help."

"But," said Bill, "you have helped me—more than I can ever tell you. You've helped me because you've listened and you didn't argue. I know that you like me, that you're my friend. You've helped me a lot. I will never forget. Good night, Jack." He walked out into the night.

Jack sat lost in thought. All of a sudden his mind went back to his own problems. To his astonishment, that which had been unclear was now clearer; that which before he could not see his way through he now saw objectively; that which had seemed to overwhelm him now seemed easier to cope with. He felt that he had more power to handle his own problems.

When you become detached mentally from yourself and concentrate on helping people with *their* difficulties, it is a fact that you will be able to cope with your own more effectively. Somehow, the act of self-giving is a personal power-releasing factor.

He Found That He Could Cope
With Anything

A great human story of coping with, perhaps, the ultimate in human problems is that of Orville E. Kelly, a newspaperman from Burlington, Iowa. He will always rank as one of my unforgettable characters. Orville Kelly has profoundly demonstrated that a person can, indeed, cope with anything, and successfully.

I first heard of Kelly in a newspaper story telling how, as a terminal case, he developed the philosophy that "death is part of life." He originated the now well-known M.T.C. (Make Today Count) program. Impressed by his sound pattern of thinking, I wrote to Mr. Kelly expressing admiration for his courageous and rational attitude. Subsequently he visited our Foundation for Christian Living where, in his sincere way of speaking, he deeply moved and inspired everyone. When he finished his talk, each of us felt that, with the same spiritual power demonstrated by Orville, we, too, could cope with anything we might have to face.

Make Today Count

Because of the widespread effects of cancer, touching as it does not only the thousands who have the disease but other thousands of loved ones who are affected, I am reprinting part of Orville Kelly's story as he wrote it for our publication, "Creative Help for Daily Living."[5] Read this human drama carefully and I'm quite sure you will think twice before again questioning the ability of a person, with God's help, to cope with anything. Here is a man who lives and deals with life on the basis of the positive principle and does it gloriously and victoriously.

> "Terminal cancer," the doctors said.
> My first reaction to this death sentence was disbelief. Such a thing could not happen to *me*, I told myself. The doctors had made a terrible mistake. But I knew they hadn't. It was true, I was going to die before my time.
> My next reaction was deep depression, a state that engulfed me for days. Thoughts of suicide even crossed my mind. And I dragged my wife and children down into a state of gloom with me. How could God have let this happen to me when everything was going well for me and my family? I was only 42 years old. I had a good job as a newspaperman and a bright future before me. We had a nice home. All of us were active and busy, and we were good churchgoing Christians. Why me?
> I would still be plunged in this kind of despair if I had not finally seen the light, accepted the Lord's way

[5]For a reprint of Orville Kelly's story, "Make Today Count," write to Foundation for Christian Living, Pawling, N.Y. 12564.

and taken positive action not only to help myself but
to also help others whose path is taking them into the
valley of death before their time.

My inner reaction was fear. Living with cancer was
a frightening experience, not only for me as a victim
but for my family, relatives and friends. My wife
Wanda, and I had not discussed it openly because I
did not want to worry her, and she had remained
silent out of fear that she would upset me. People
stopped dropping in to see us because it was too
depressing for them.

I began to understand that it was the prospect of
death that frightened me, not the thought of having
cancer. That is when depression—despair—took hold
of my life. Wanda was under a physician's care for a
severe case of nerves. The situation reached its low
point as we were driving home one day from Iowa
City after a session of chemotherapy. It was a
beautiful fall day, but as I glanced toward my wife,
I saw a look of complete dejection on her face. We
drove silently across the prairie.

He Takes Positive Action

Finally I decided something had to be done, and
fast, to help Wanda accept my fate. It was then I
found myself looking again to God for guidance. I
asked for His help. Then I turned to Wanda.

"Let's talk about it," I said. "I'm going to die from
cancer unless something else kills me, but I'm not
dead yet. So let's start enjoying life again." I told her
that we should explain the situation to the children
since they already knew something was wrong, and
that we should face my terminal illness as a family in a
positive way. We went home and told the children. It
wasn't easy, but I did tell them.

There are those who might wonder about this
approach to death. I felt I had nothing to lose and
everything to gain by trying the simple thought of
making each day count. After all, none of us *really*
know when we are going to die. We are all "terminal"
in a sense.

Family life gradually returned to normal; not perfect, but normal. All of us realized that things would never be completely all right again, but we learned that it is possible to live with cancer instead of just giving up. My new philosophy could be summed up simply: "Each day I will accept not as another day closer to death, but as another day of life. I accept each day as a gift from God to be appreciated, enjoyed and lived to its fullest."

This new attitude gave me a renewed interest in life, and I began writing again. I started by doing an article for our local newspaper in which I advocated the formation of an organization of terminally ill patients who could meet informally to help one another cope with their problems in a positive way.

The telephone began ringing as soon as the article appeared. People called to tell me that they had gone through the same emotional crisis I had faced. So many called that I invited them to what became the first meeting of the organization we called "Make Today Count." Eighteen people attended, among them cancer victims, relatives of terminal patients, ministers, nurses and nursing students. I made it clear that no one was to cry on anyone's shoulder or try to gain sympathy for his suffering. We were there to seek positive ways to make the rest of our lives more meaningful.

Nearly 50 attended our third meeting. Make Today Count was described in news-agency feature articles and on radio and television. This brought letters pouring in from people who wanted to start chapters in their home towns. Some who wrote were not physically ill, just depressed; they saw in Make Today Count the possibility of improving their lives. Chapters have been established in many states and abroad.

Meetings are informal, unstructured, and there are no chapter officers. Just bringing people together to talk and share their problems over coffee can accomplish a great deal. Through our conversations we are learning to accept the idea that death is part of life.

Live for Today

During the period when I was severely depressed, I was being treated efficiently and with kindness and sympathy by the physicians who had pronounced the death sentence. Ministers discussed life after death. But no one seemed to mention living for today!

I'll have to admit that though I may be helping others through Make Today Count, I am also helping myself. I have stopped measuring time in months and years. Seconds are the framework in which I operate. The trace of a smile on my wife's face, the laughter of my children, a flash of sunlight. They are of the moment, and of a lifetime.

Of course my wife and I dreamed of growing old together, but we have learned that life is fragile and unpredictable for everyone. Of course I didn't want to have cancer, but I didn't have any choice. So I say to myself, "What do I have to lose by trying to be happy?"

Some people have achieved immortality through their art or through acts of heroism or nobility. Since I am neither especially talented nor heroic, facing death has been especially difficult. The fear and uncertainty that confronted me when I learned I had terminal cancer were worse than the idea of death itself. Looking back to those first days of shock, I know now that my family and I grieved about a death that had not yet occurred. But by discussing death and being open about cancer and its problems, I have found myself more concerned with life than with death.

In other words, until we realize that death is a part of life, I don't think we can truly enjoy life. Because I feel that way, when a man recently said to me, "We have something in common; we are both dying of cancer," I was able to reply, "No, we have in common the fact that we are both still alive."

The other day a little girl at school remarked to my nine-year-old daughter, "I saw your daddy on TV and he is dying of cancer, isn't he?"

"Yes," my daughter replied, "but he's not dead yet!"

Not by a long shot. Today is where I am and today I am alive. I am not especially concerned about yesterday or tomorrow. I am concerned about *today* . . . right now! I am trying to make time count.

New Awareness of Life

Looking back, I find it difficult to believe today that I am the same person who blamed God for my cancer and who doubted His existence. Perhaps, in my case, death made me aware of life.

One night when I found it difficult to sleep, I wrote a prayer. It goes like this:

Our Heavenly Father . . .
Give me the strength to face each night
Before the dawn.
Give me the courage to watch my children at play,
And my wife at my side,
Without a trace of sorrow in my smile;
Let me count each passing moment,
As I once marked the fleeting days and nights,
And give me hope for each tomorrow.
Let my dreams be dreams of the future.
But when life on earth is over,
Let there be no sadness,
But only joy, for the golden days I've had.
Amen.

You have read the profound philosophy and faith of a man who is demonstrating in a practical way that one can cope with anything. You have read a sound, in-depth description of life at a top level of victory. This is the vibrant positive principle in action.

My wife, Ruth, and I had lunch with Orville and Wanda and other friends one golden autumn day when the maple- and oak-covered hills of Dutchess County were at their height of glorious coloring. We sat in a restaurant by the side of a highway with heavy traffic going by. But beyond the highway was a meadow and beyond that the hills, and in the meadow cows were grazing.

Orville looked beyond the traffic to the cattle and the meadow and the hills in their dress of red and gold, and with misty eyes said, "What is so beautiful as cows grazing peacefully in an autumn landscape?" He was silent for a moment, then said musingly, "This morning coming down from Connecticut I saw a red bird sitting on a fence post. It looked so bright and happy. I think I shall always remember that bird on a fence post one bright morning in Connecticut."

His were not the only eyes that were misty as he spoke. All of us around the table in that busy restaurant became keenly aware of the triumphant life of our friend. Actually, we became conscious of God at that moment, who can make a human being into a victorious spirit. So please believe it, for it is true. You can cope with anything—you really can.

What suggestions have been made in this chapter to help you cope?

1. Take life and its problems with your two hands.
2. Then put your hands in God's hands.
3. Remember that God will see you through anything, so stay close to Him.
4. Keep unperturbed—never panic. Be a philosopher. Think, always think. Do not react emotionally. Use your head; think. You will find that you can cope.
5. Always believe that you can, and you will find that you can.
6. Help other people to cope with their problems and your own will be easier to cope with.
7. Always— Make Today Count.

TENTH
WAY TO KEEP
THE POSITIVE
PRINCIPLE GOING

The Fabulous Secret of Energy and Vitality Thinking

"If we did all the things we are capable of doing we would literally astonish ourselves." So said the great inventive genius and thinker Thomas A. Edison.

Did you ever astonish yourself? Did I? Embarrassing but provocative question, isn't it? But if we potentially possess all that capacity—and it must be so if as great an authority as Edison says so—then the question is How may it be released? I have discovered that one way to release the potential of an individual is to activate the fabulous secret of energy and vitality. Add to that an underscoring of the positive principle, and any person can become altogether different; indeed, very different.

A physician asked me to see a man whom he rather inelegantly described as "rolling in money" but who was completely out of energy and vitality. "I can continue to pamper him and feed him pills, but that kind of treatment doesn't jibe with my idea of ethical medicine. He isn't really ill, but his thinking sure is diseased. He is a person of real ability, but it is far from operative. How about taking a crack at this guy? Maybe your kind of medicine will do him some good." So ended the breezy case history by a doctor who nevertheless had pretty keen insights not only into human disability but also into psychological reactions.

175

I See the De-energized Patient

When I arrived at his sumptuous apartment, the man went into a long and detailed account of his ill feelings of mind and body and how weak, depleted and absolutely down he felt. "I used to have lots of drive and go," he declared feebly, "but now I have no more energy than a cat." Which I thought an inaccurate comparison inasmuch as all the cats I know, while they may act lazy, can leap up and spring like a bullet out of a gun.

As he talked I recalled the wise advice of my good doctor friend, Dr. Z. T. Bercovitz, to the effect that "to get in tone it is necessary to get in tune." So I said, "Look, I'm not a medical doctor, as you know, but I try to serve as a kind of doctor of the mind, and perhaps the soul, too. And a good many medical men believe that not a few feelings of physical illness and depletion take their rise in diseased mental and spiritual attitudes."

He rather blinked at that one and went off on a lengthy description of his mother and father, "always poor in this world's goods, but great Christians. Yes, sir, real Christians. In church every Sunday," et cetera, et cetera.

"Well," I responded, "what they were may have no bearing on what you are, but, incidentally, have you any evidence that their piety rubbed off on you?"

He began to get the point, for in replying to that question he said, "Guess you've got me there. Got to admit I'm pretty much of a heel; been through every sin in the book. You wrote a book on positive thinking, but you're looking at the biggest negative thinker in this town. Tell me what you are going to do about that."

"It isn't what I'm going to do, but what are *you* going to do? Mope around here thinking negative thoughts

176

and being pseudo-sick the rest of your life? How old are you, by the way?"

"I'm fifty-two years of age and I've had it."

By this time I was liking this man more by the minute, for underneath it all he was basically honest and forthright. And he had brainpower, too; that was not to be denied. Indeed, he had the makings of a real, honest-to-goodness, healthy man.

"Look," I said, "what do you say we drain off all that mental and spiritual infection that is sapping your energy and leaving your whole system tired and devitalized?"

Perhaps unconsciously he had wanted this kind of treatment, for he began to open up and come clean. It was hard for him at first to discuss intimate matters with a stranger, but I guess he trusted me as a pastor, for he began to pour out a mass of sick thinking and unhealthy action that went back to his youth. He had an enormous sense of guilt, and despite his bombastic demeanor he was, surprisingly, filled with quite a lot of inadequacy and inferiority attitudes.

Finally he asked, rather piteously, if I thought God would forgive him. "Why not ask Him?" I suggested.

"You mean now? I never prayed in public before."

"Oh, I'm not the public, just your friend. So go on, ask Him to forgive you."

That he did in slow and hesitant words, but with great sincerity. "What did you feel the Lord say to you?" I asked.

With a sense of wonder and a very relieved kind of look, he said, "I'm forgiven, I really feel I'm forgiven. I remember He promised that all you have to do is to ask and He hears and forgives. But still I don't feel as peaceful as I expected."

"You've got one thing more to do, or maybe two things. The first is to forgive yourself. You see," I continued, "we all have a built-in censor which tells us we must be punished for evils we have done. And that censor is pretty difficult to call off. But you have had your share of self-inflicted punishment, so now say aloud, 'I hereby forgive myself even as God has forgiven me.'"

"That," he declared upon repeating the statement, "makes sense—a great big lot of sense."

"Okay," I said, "the second thing is to believe that in the name of the Lord and of yourself [I remembered the doctor's diagnosis] you are a well man. Really believe that. Now get up and get out of here and get going." He took me to the door, gave me a crushing handclasp that was vastly different from the flabby hand he had extended earlier. "Keep that good old positive principle going," I admonished.

"Sure will," he declared. "Just watch me and see."

I did watch him and I did see. A week later I called on the telephone to inquire about him and found that he was back on the job and going strong. And he kept going with continuous vitality and enthusiasm.

I do not want it to be inferred from this rapid get-well story that I am any healer or that such cases always work out so immediately. Actually, in a sense, the man healed himself through complete surrender to God. And he continued re-energized and revitalized for some twenty years, for I often saw him in our congregation at the Marble Collegiate Church. As he told me, "I'm on the mental and spiritual beam and will never get off it again." He kept that promise until he died in an accident at age seventy-three.

The incident was enlightening and educational for me, too, for it showed the powerful effect on bodily reactions of an unhealthy pattern of thought. Many times since that experience I have done a rehabilitation job on my own thoughts when I found myself tired or run-down or in any sense de-energized. Unconsciously we can have a mental buildup of sick thinking which may result in debilitating or even serious illness. Certainly it can reduce efficiency. The fabulous secret of energy and vitality thinking should be used in activating the positive principle. And invariably the result is renewable personality force.

Contact the Life Force

It was in the writing of Myrtle Fillmore, who with her husband founded the Unity School of Christianity, that I first became aware of the important life force concept. This is based on the principle that we were not created and endowed with vital life only to have it at once start to decline. The truth is that we can constantly be in a re-creative process through which the powerful life force is ever renewing vitality. I have observed that those who practice the fabulous secret of energy and vitality thinking keep vibrant power going amazingly despite all of those enemies of well-being which tend to deplete strength.

Over the years of an extremely active schedule of writing, speaking, editing, publishing and administering, I have kept my own energy and vitality going by constant affirmation of the life force, visualizing it as continuously flowing through mind and body. This practice has steadily renewed strength and kept an unimpeded flow of energy operating without diminution. Certainly I become tired, but it is never a tiredness that a good night's sleep will not cure. My particular job requires keeping a number of balls in the air at the same time, so to speak, and being called upon daily to make decisions in a variety of fields. And always there is the necessity to keep

179

producing. Since without energy and vitality no active person can sustain a vigorous program, it is a matter of utmost importance to learn how to keep it going.

The Way a Doctor Kept It Going

In my early years in New York when I was constantly gearing up to an ever increasing schedule and experiencing the tension that often accompanies such driving activity, I became a friend of the late Dr. William Seaman Bainbridge, who practiced medicine on Gramercy Park in Manhattan. He was an extraordinarily busy man, not only in his own profession but in many societies and organizations, in which he was inevitably a leader.

One day I gave a vigorous talk to the New York Rotary Club, of which he was president and I a member. These meetings are scheduled to close promptly at 1:45 P.M., for the Rotarians are all business and professional men who have schedules to keep. Dr. Bainbridge, who always had an office full of patients waiting for him, scheduled his first afternoon appointment for two o'clock. "Come on, Norman," he said hurriedly, "let's grab a cab and go downtown together. I want you to stop by my office for five minutes on the way to your office." At 1:50 we arrived at his old brownstone on Gramercy Park and went into his private office. Outside in the waiting room was a formidable lineup of patients.

"That was a great talk you gave at Rotary," he said. "You sure did pour it on. You are bound to be on a high tension level and so am I, and we've got to cool it. Let's relax and get the old energy and vitality going to compensate for the big expenditure of energy we have been making." So saying, he flopped into a big chair, his legs straight out, arms hanging limply over the sides of the

180

chair and head back against the headrest. "Do the same," he directed, and I flopped down similarly.

After a minute of silence he said, "Peace and quietness are filling our minds. Renewal is now taking place in our physical bodies. We are now being re-created in every part of our beings. We are being given energy control sufficient for our needs." Another moment of silence followed this impressive affirmation. Then, "Okay, now we're ready to begin a busy afternoon. That's a prescription for you, my friend," he concluded in his kindly fashion. Whereupon he called for his first patient and I went out into the hectic city of New York "raring to go." I have faithfully followed the doctor's method for re-energizing oneself since he taught it to me over thirty years ago.

The Way an Ambassador Kept It Going

Lawrence Townsend, once Ambassador to Austria and other countries, was a tall, lithe, vigorous man up into his nineties. His erect carriage bespoke military training as a young man. He had all the graciousness and savoir faire associated with traditional ambassadors and was a close friend of the late King George V and Queen Mary. I knew him quite well in his later years and visited him one day in his Florida home.

I found him in his "place of meditation" in his spacious garden. This was an enclosure done in stained wood somewhat like a log cabin, with no top, being entirely open to the sun. He was in bathing trunks and I noticed that his skin was tight, his body muscular, fat-free and tanned. His eyes were bright and his face was wreathed in smiles as he greeted me. "Excuse this informal welcome, but I'm performing my daily vitality and energy ritual. It's this practice that has kept me going strong over the long pull," he explained. "Excuse me a moment while I get dressed and then we will visit and have lunch."

"No, Lawrence, don't stop. I could use a good vitality and energy ritual myself. Please let me watch your procedure." Thus encouraged, and being an avid believer in affirmative processes, Mr. Townsend said, "Okay, here it is." He then stood straight up, "reaching for the sky with the crown of my head," as he put it. By such reaching he drew every organ into place and counteracted the sag that mars the physical form of so many of us. He then raised his arms high and reached for the sky with his fingers. Then followed a rather usual type of exercising and I could see the strong muscles rippling under the skin.

"So much for the physical part of it," he said, breathing easily, with no puffing or other sign of exertion. "Now for the more important mental and spiritual exercise." Still standing erect and tall, he said something like the following, which I copied word for word at the time and practiced so often that, while the written formula has long since disappeared, it remains in memory. "Lord God Almighty, my Creator and Heavenly Father, as the sun from heaven shines upon and renews my body, so does the sunshine of Your great Spirit warm my mind and my soul, renewing me by the power of Your wondrous grace." He used the old stately terms most impressively. "I am now emptying from my mind every thought, idea and memory that is not in harmony with Your goodness. I hereby drop from consciousness every selfish, evil and unworthy thought. I let go all uncharitable attitudes, every fear and every vestige of ill will and resentment. As my mind is now emptied and clean of every unhealthy thought, You are now filling it with thoughts of goodness, love and faith. Thank You, dear Lord, for I can feel at this moment Your freshening and renewing power. And it feels so wonderfully good! Thank You, thank You."

Formula of Thanksgiving

To this he added what he called "the formula of thanksgiving." Still standing tall, he said, "Thank You, O Creator, for my wonderful body which only You can make; for my strong heart, my good stomach, my healthy liver; for my keen eyes, my sensitive ears and my brain; all parts of my body are now serving me as well as when I was a youth. Then, Heavenly Father, thank You for that immortal part of me, my soul, which I place once again in Your keeping. I affirm my desire to serve You all the days of my life until evening falls and I enter into rest and on into eternal life, still with You whom I have loved always. Thank You for Your gracious forgiveness and for the peace of mind You are giving me every day all the way."

I stood entranced, admiring this unusual man. Some might regard what I have just described as an oddball kind of thing, but I assure you this man was as sharp as they make them; a highly innovative and effective personality. He lived as a strong, healthy man until about age ninety-five, then one night he lay down to sleep and did not awaken in this mortal world.

But I have little doubt that on that next morning in some brighter and more beautiful place of meditation he was still practicing his ritual of energy and vitality thinking. Many to whom I have suggested this procedure have testified to its efficacy. I often do it myself, and it works wonders in the energy renewal process. You can perform it right in your own home even without sunshine. That can be mentally induced. Every organ in the body will respond and you will feel good.

Try this aspect of the positive principle and keep it going, for it will keep you going.

Don't Drag Through Life

It is a pathetic fact that multitudes of people actually drag through life in a dreary sort of way, having little or none of the zest and enthusiasm which should normally characterize a human being. And the big majority of such people probably have nothing really wrong physically. But they handle the duties and responsibilities of life in a halfhearted and desultory manner, just getting by. When a person is only getting by, it is a fact that he is not really getting with it. Under such circumstances life can, of necessity, be only partial; the good-better-best that it should be just does not come through.

But when a person of this type has a real energizing and vitalizing experience, he is astounded by the powerful new quality of life which changes everything for him. Thomas A. Edison's statement previously mentioned spectacularly applies: "If we did all the things we are capable of doing we would literally astonish ourselves." So it pays to find and practice the fabulous secret of energy and vitality thinking. Those old, tired, desultory feelings will be eliminated by a surging infusion of new interest, zest and enthusiasm.

Run-down Career Woman

An incident of personal energy renewal I very much like to recount concerns a brilliant and hard-driving New York City career woman, a great friend of Mrs. Peale's and mine. This super-energetic person finally cracked under the unreasonable and uncontrolled pace and suffered a nervous breakdown which took the form of complete drainage of energy and vitality. Formerly dynamic, she was now listless and weary. She would sit staring ahead, uncaring and disinterested, sadly deteriorated in spirit; indeed, completely changed from the excited and competent person she had been.

Her doctor suggested a change of scene and she went off to a seaside resort where she wandered about disconsolately or sat drained and apathetic. Then she took to going to the beach, not to swim but to sit or lie indolently on the sand. It was during the off season and the beach was practically her own. She welcomed the loneliness, for this formerly gregarious person now avoided people; it was too tiring to try to talk with anyone.

Even though the weather was growing colder, she spent many days on the beach. She liked the stimulating crispness. One day she suddenly began to pray, and in depth. She was a religious person with a leaning toward scientific spiritual truth, and she believed in the reality of Divine healing as not being inconsistent with medical treatment. She began to pray specifically for the healing of her condition. Presently she had a strangely certain feeling that her prayer was being granted.

And it came about in a curious manner. One day as she lay on the beach amid some tall beach grass, she found herself listening to the sound of the surf; and as she listened intently she noticed a regularity of rhythm in the surging of the sea on the shore. Then her eye caught a single blade of beach grass moving gracefully in the gentle breeze. As she watched she began to note that it, too, moved in rhythm, and the wind that moved the beach grass was also rhythmical. It occurred to her to take her own pulse and, astonishingly, it also possessed rhythm not unlike that of the sea and the beach grass and the wind.

Impressed by this phenomenon, she meditated on the fascinating reality upon which she had stumbled. Was it true that all nature is in rhythm, including her own being? Could this be the answer to her intense prayer for healing? She caught herself thinking those familiar words, "God moves in a mysterious way His wonders to perform."[1] Suddenly a healing thought flashed up in consciousness. Her trouble was that she had got out of rhythm in her thinking. As a result she could no longer work easily; there was too much overtense drive and not enough controlled emotional relaxation. "What I need is that wonderful thing called 'the peace of God, which passeth all understanding.' "[2] Now she was on the way to recovery, intuitively realizing that renewal of body would follow renewal of mind and spirit. Gradually, with consistent practice of the rhythmic principle, she discovered the secret of energy and vitality thinking and experienced a full return of health and vigor.

Because it illustrates the positive principle and a truth technique of wholeness and orderly personality organization, I like this true story and have often told it to people in similar condition. It carries with it a profound and practical truth principle: Get into rhythm with nature, with yourself, with your job, with other people and with God, and you will truly know the joyous fullness of life. Nor is it necessary to go to some lonely beach and lie on the sand to achieve a result. This process of renewal of energy and vitality can be employed where you are and at any time, for it is an exercise in mental therapy.

Never let yourself be driven or agitated to such an extent that the rhythmic flow of personality gets off center. An important procedure for you and for me and for all of us in this modern, high-strung world of tensed-up people is to keep working in rhythmic harmony with the fabulous secret of energy and vitality

[1] Olney Hymns (1779), No. 35, by William Cowper.
[2] Philippians 4:7.

thinking. Every day spend some unhurried moments in thinking energy, thinking vitality, actually "seeing" the life force at work in you. By thus emphasizing and underscoring such a creative operational experience, your energy and vitality will continue on and on and still on. You will keep the positive principle ever working for you.

I Know These Energy Principles Work

It is with complete assurance that I advocate these principles of energy and vitality thinking to my readers, for I have applied them successfully in my own personal experience. Indeed, nothing in this book is theoretically presented, for all of its principles have been tested both by me personally and by persons in whose integrity and honest judgment I have the greatest confidence.

Over a six-month period I carried out a weight-reduction program, taking off substantial poundage in the process. All went well until I began to experience periods of weakness and a startling diminution of energy, with a corresponding reduction of vitality. Inasmuch as I had always enjoyed a seemingly boundless supply of energy and vitality, this new feeling of weakness was disturbing, even bewildering. I was advised to change my diet to include some items in moderation which had been eliminated to effect the weight loss. But, having worked assiduously to take off the pounds, I was not about to take the chance of putting some back on again.

Medication to upgrade energy was prescribed. I took an energy-producing pill for a few mornings and it did have some effect. But then I decided that I did not want to get increased energy by the use of drugs, however innocuous. Accordingly, on the assumption that my problem was basically mental in nature, I began a regular routine of visualizing or imaging myself as having my old-time energy in full measure. Daily I practiced energy affirmations, declaring that the life force was revitalizing my mind and my body. I affirmed the value, in health terms, of the reduced weight and that my entire system was responding with new vigor. The effect of this procedure became increasingly noticeable with each passing day. The dramatically reduced diet was continued, weight was reduced to a new low level, but the weak feeling passed off and my usual energetic vitality pattern returned in full measure.

There are, of course, cases of energy loss in which the cause is basically physical in nature, in which event medical treatment employing medication is indicated. When loss of energy occurs, one should consult a physician and faithfully carry out prescribed treatment. But even in such cases it would seem that mental treatment would serve as an aid in the recuperative process. And along with the medical and mental approach, the application of spiritual therapy can hardly fail to have a salutary effect. Indeed, I know of one doctor who, in cases of energy loss, adds to his regular prescription a verbal "spiritual prescription." He advises his patient to pass daily through the mind the following words, which he says he has known to effect recuperation: "They that wait upon the Lord shall renew their strength; they shall mount up with wings as eagles; they shall run, and not be weary; and they shall walk, and not faint."[3] That affirming of the positive principle is a viable energy-producing agent.

Motivation Ended Inertia

At a national trade association meeting where I addressed the delegates at their annual convention ban-

[3] Isaiah 40:31.

quet, I spoke on the subject of why positive thinkers get positive results. Following my talk, a man asked if he could speak to me about a matter that seemed to be bothering him considerably. He appeared to be about forty-five years old, but, to my surprise, said he was thirty-five, or ten years younger than I had guessed. The older aspect was conveyed by a drawn look on his face and a pronounced slump of the shoulders. He rather gave the impression of a person slowly recovering from an illness, and he appeared to be low in spirit.

As we sat in the hotel lobby he explained that he just wasn't getting anywhere and that he didn't enjoy his job anymore. His job, it appeared, was an executive type position, neither at the bottom nor at the top, and he remarked glumly, "One thing is sure—I never expect to go any further in the business. I've hit my top."

"Why not?" I asked. "And what is your 'top'?"

"Oh," he replied in a weary and depressed tone, "nobody thinks very much of me. They know I haven't much on the ball. I've been written off. It's a wonder they don't fire me. Wouldn't blame them if they did."

"Ever come up with any new ideas, any fresh, innovative suggestions? Are you really on the company team? Do you show an interest in what goes on? Are you pulling full strength on your oar?"

"Oh, no, I never have any ideas, and so how can I be innovative? And besides, I'm a slow starter in the morning and never get going very strong at any time."

Suspecting the possibility of a physical problem, I asked if he had a medical checkup and it seemed that he had come through such examination successfully except that the doctor had commented on a general sluggishness. But beyond that his health seemed passable.

Then he rather took me aback. "I hate to tell you," he said rather diffidently, "but I read your book, *Enthusiasm Makes the Difference*, and it really teed me off,

189

got me all steamed up, and for a while I went places. I did, for a fact. But then that enthusiasm began to leak, and just look at me now!"

When I asked what happened to cause the leak, he began to tell me of a few blows and setbacks. "They really threw me," he admitted.

"But you see, my friend," I explained, "it just isn't a real, bona fide enthusiasm if it can't stand up to a few blows or even to a lot of shock. Enthusiasm isn't only for fair weather and easy going. Almost anyone can keep it going when all is fortuitous. It is when the setbacks come—and it is the nature of setbacks not to come singly but in bunches—that enthusiasm needs to go to work. It is designed to give you the lift you need when things are tough. Guess you didn't read the book all that perceptively, or perhaps I didn't convey this idea to you with clarity. You must have another go at that enthusiasm. You know what the word means, do you not? It is derived from *entheos*—Greek for 'God in you.' So may I suggest that you need more of God in you."

"But how is that done? Frankly, I do not understand. I'm a now-and-then kind of churchgoing man. A believer, but I guess I never got with it, at least in the terms you are using."

I tried to explain that there exists a powerful energizing force in the spiritual life principle. All energy began with the Creator, who infused it not only in all natural processes, but also into that higher form of nature called human nature. The more closely, then, that a person identifies with the Creator, the more surely he will experience within his own nature the process of re-creation which operates in all creation. The individual who has permitted himself to run down in spirit can be renewed by returning in mind to the Creator, whose function it is to re-create as well as to create. I quoted a Bible passage which bears on this type of reasoning: "In

Him we live, and move, and have our being."[4] That is to say, in the Creator and Re-creator we live (have vitality) and move (have energy) and have our being (function as a well-organized person).

That was all the time I had to talk. We shook hands and parted. He kept in touch, however. He went home and happened to tell one of his friends about our conversation and was surprised to hear that he, too, had been down the same road but had found the answer that changed his attitudes and so changed him. He took our man to a businessmen's weekly breakfast, a spiritually oriented meeting, where he was warmly welcomed. As he told me later, "Those men, all of them leaders in our town, had a quality of life I'd never seen before. Through their kindly understanding, after some weeks of attending these meetings, I finally did as you suggested and in my own way I'm sure that I have found the Power. That old enthusiasm is really coming back. It's surprising how this new motivation is ridding me of that inertia that was taking me down the failure road."

This man changed his depressed thought pattern by using the fabulous secret of energy and vitality thinking. He found the positive principle, and now has learned how to keep it going.

He Got His Mental Attitude Healed

I watched Gary Nolan, a star pitcher for the Cincinnati Reds National League baseball team, as he pitched brilliantly in the deciding play-off game of the 1975 season with the Pittsburgh Pirates. But before Gary Nolan could clinch this victory over a powerful challenging team, he had first to achieve a personal victory over negative thinking. The following newspaper story,

[4]Acts 17:28.

given here verbatim, very well describes the process of mind control which preceded the arm control of this great pitcher. He discovered the secret of energy and vitality through application of the positive principle. But read the news account[5] for yourself:

> Fireballing pitcher Gary Nolan credits Dr. Norman Vincent Peale and his "Power of Positive Thinking" philosophy with salvaging his baseball career.
>
> Nolan admits he was ready to give up the game at age 26 before Dr. Peale's words inspired him to make a dramatic comeback.
>
> Nolan was a star righthander for the Cincinnati Reds before the All-Star Game in 1972, compiling a sensational 12-3 record.
>
> But he soon developed shoulder problems that have plagued him ever since.
>
> He developed an unusually large bone spur. It rubbed painfully against his finely conditioned muscles. Things got so bad that Nolan announced his retirement midway through the 1974 season.
>
> But surgery during the winter and help from a book written by Dr. Peale have returned him to the starting rotation.
>
> "I was lower than a snake's belly," Nolan said.
>
> "But that was until I was reminded of the guy who felt sorry for himself because he had no shoes and then met up with a guy who had no legs."
>
> At the depths of despair but still hoping to regain the form that earned him recognition as one of the top pitchers in the National League, he submitted to the surgeon's scalpel.
>
> It was a reluctant choice.
>
> "I didn't want to have it," Nolan said. "It was purely psychological. Mention surgery around any pitcher, and everyone hushes up."
>
> But the operation was a success. Doctors removed the spur, but not the impression of two years of pitching failure that it had left on Nolan's mind.
>
> It was then that he came in contact with the book by

[5]By Marty Gunther, from *The National Tattler*.

Peale, one of the leading exponents of man's ability to overcome even the greatest odds with the right frame of mind.

"I borrowed it from Tony Cloninger, a former teammate," Nolan said. "He got it when he went to Peale for help. He gave it to me at a point when all of my confidence was gone.

"It stressed the power of positive thinking and inner strength."

Nolan read the words carefully and captured the full impact of Peale's message. His self-confidence returned. It has shown in his game.

With one-third of the season behind him, the 27-year-old hurler is among the top 15 in the league in allowing fewest runs per innings pitched.

And the Reds are leading the Los Angeles Dodgers, their arch rivals and 1974 pennant winners, by a comfortable margin.

Cincinnati Manager Sparky Anderson has received unseen pitching help at the hands of Norman Vincent Peale.

Summing up the tenth way to keep the positive principle going:

1. Learn the fabulous secret of energy and vitality thinking.
2. Empty the mind of all unhealthy thoughts, replacing them with wholesome, creative concepts.
3. Visualize the life force continuously at work within you, refreshing body, mind and spirit.
4. Affirm daily—more than once—that you are now renewing energy and vitality.
5. Get into harmony with the basic rhythm of life which the Creator set in motion.
6. Remember Edison's remark: "If we did all the things we are capable of doing we would literally astonish ourselves."
7. Astonish yourself!
8. Always keep your mental attitudes healthy.
9. Relate all activity to the positive principle and keep going strong every day all the way.

ELEVENTH
WAY TO KEEP
THE POSITIVE
PRINCIPLE GOING

In-Depth Faith Always Wins Over Difficulties

As the roller coaster car reached the summit of its steep climb and began the downward swoop with rapidly increasing speed, the young boy became terrified. Wildly he envisioned the careening car flying off the track, killing everyone aboard. In acute fear he gripped the bar in front of him. The father, sensing his son's reaction, put a strong arm around him, hugging him close. Assured by this evidence of protection, the boy's terror came under control.

Victory Over Fear

Many years after this incident in a midwestern amusement park, the boy, now a man of twenty-five, was exposed to a much more intense fear experience. This time he found an in-depth faith that not only sustained him but actually gave him freedom from fear forever. Jerry Adams told his exciting and moving story as we drove to the airport one morning after I had addressed a meeting in his city. We had been discussing the important place of faith in successful living, and the subject of destructive fear came up. He quietly made the statement that he was no longer affected by fear, that he felt certain he would never be afraid again, either in life or in death. This was said with calm assurance and with a complete lack of bravado. It was evident that Jerry Adams had attained that in-depth quality of faith which eliminates all fear. He had achieved the faith that wins over difficulties.

Being deeply interested in any human victory over fear, that greatest of all adversaries, I asked the reason for his sturdily expressed conviction. It developed from an incident that happened on the U.S.S. *Oriskany*, an aircraft carrier, off the coast of Vietnam.

As a bombardier/navigator Jerry was flying two missions daily over enemy territory. Twice every day his plane was catapulted into the air. This is not exactly the most calming experience, as I know personally, having myself been catapulted from the deck of the U.S.S. *Kitty Hawk*. Over North Vietnam Jerry and his comrades faced the danger of antiaircraft fire. And on each return the men had to find that little speck of landing deck in the wide expanse of sea. All of this provided plenty of opportunity for fear to take over. But Jerry's chief dread was that of being shot down and captured by a reputedly ruthless enemy.

Most Terrifying Experience

Then came the most terrifying experience of all, but one in which he found the boon of complete deliverance from fear. Jerry's bomber crew was made up of Lieutenant Commander Richard Walls and Lieutenant (j.g.) Ignatius Signorelli, plus an ensign going along as a passenger to Saigon. A bomber blast-off is always an awesome experience, the object being to hurl thirty-five tons of aircraft into the air from a standstill position to a speed of two hundred miles an hour in only 150 feet of deck.

The crew was checked out and ready to go. Heads back against headrests, the men were waiting for the powerful thrust of the catapult. The noise increased to terrific volume, pressure swelled, the aircraft screamed against the restraining cables. The boy who had been afraid on that midwestern roller coaster so long ago sat awaiting the thrust of the catapult that would send them off on another mission. But instead of the routine takeoff came a sharp jolt and a crash, metal crunching and ripping all around. The wreck of the aircraft slid down the deck and over the edge, plunging wildly one hundred feet, or the equivalent of ten stories, down into the sea, with the men trapped inside.

On this tragic fall into the ocean, the certainty of death flashed into Jerry's mind. But then also came the overwhelming conviction that he was not alone. He had an awareness of the presence of Jesus, feeling that presence keenly and without any doubt. He knew instantly that whether it was to be life or death, he would be taken care of. He seemed to feel around him the strong arm of a Heavenly Father, and there was no panic. There was no fear.

Plunging from the great height of the carrier deck, he and his companions were driven perhaps fifty feet deep into the water. It grew darker and darker the farther down he sank. Struggling to locate the escape hatch, he found there was no cockpit; there was nothing left. He was still strapped in his seat, and something, doubtless a part of the wrecked aircraft, dragged at his feet. This made him wonder whether he would ever reach the surface of the water again, since there was no real feeling in either leg. Then the realization came that both legs had been broken. Responding automatically to his survival training, he freed himself of his lap and shoulder harness, inflated his Mae West and, lungs screaming for air, shot up to the surface. He saw the massive bulk of the *Oriskany* only a few feet away. It swept by so closely that he was under the overhang of the great ship. The captain had swung the carrier around, thus protecting the men in the sea from the ship's gigantic screws. All of them were rescued. Jerry, hoisted by helicopter, passed out from incredible pain. After twelve months in the hospital and several operations, he was able to walk again. But as he finished his dramatic story, he repeated, "I know now that the Lord is always near and I shall never fear again. And when death finally does come, I shall not be afraid, for He will be there to take care of me."

This man had come upon one of the greatest of all facts in this life. Perhaps it is the supreme fact; that we are not alone. In his near-death experience he discovered that ultimate value called in-depth faith, the kind of faith that wins over all difficulties. Before this experience he had been a regular churchgoer and as a boy had been trained in Sunday School. But this was different —this was a new faith in depth. It brought to him a profound and unshakable assurance and absolute certainty, without any doubt whatsoever, that, in this world or the next, there is nothing to be afraid of, for always the Father's protecting arm is around you.

Bigger Than Your Difficulties

This experience of the positive principle leads to the realization that you are bigger than your difficulties. No matter how menacing, how formidable, how terribly awesome they may be, you possess the potential power to stand up to difficulties and overcome them, all of them. And the potential to which we refer is in-depth faith, the greatest power available to a human being, the force by which you can move mountains of difficulty. Remember what the Bible says on this subject? "If ye have faith, and doubt not, . . . ye shall say unto this mountain, Be thou removed, and be thou cast into the sea; it shall be done."[1]

But the kind of faith able to accomplish such extraordinary feats is an extra-real type of belief, a down-deep attitude that never accepts defeat. It is an intensity of belief, an intensity of positive attitude, an intensity of faith in God, of faith in life and of faith in yourself. It is a powerful concept embedded in consciousness, really embedded in the inner essence of the mind, that, when needed, will marshal powerful creative forces to your aid. And so strong is this belief that it will admit of no doubt, no doubt whatsoever. Indeed, doubt has no effect upon intense faith, upon faith of in-depth quality.

Of course this is not to say that no doubt ever intrudes. There are times when doubt comes to everyone, and it can be grim indeed, darkening the mind with discouraging negatives. But the difference between having no faith or a bland, formal-like faith and an in-depth faith is that doubts bombard the latter futilely. Such faith is impervious to doubt and so presently the attack of doubt ends and the practitioner of intense faith proceeds to handle his difficulties victoriously. He exerts his power to keep the positive principle going.

Doubtless the question at once arises as to how the average individual can cultivate a faith of this in-depth quality. And of course the answer is to develop God-conditioned attitudes or, to put it another way, to grow in God-consciousness to such an extent that mentally, at all times and under whatever conditions, any frightening difficulties simply do not frighten you or have any power over you. But this again may seem incredible until one undertakes to develop intensity of belief through practice and through a mental buildup of faith attitudes.

[1]Matthew 21:21.

Once in Alberta, Canada, I gave a talk at a Chamber of Commerce annual dinner. It was a large and enthusiastic crowd and in the speech I developed my concepts of positive thinking. Afterward, while shaking hands with the people, a man breezed up; no other expression can quite convey his demeanor and attitude of joy, enthusiasm and obvious aliveness. In a few sentences, delivered rapidly and with force, he gave me one of the most valuable mental-overcoming formulas I have ever heard. Other people in line were pressing forward, and he spoke so succinctly and swiftly that he was gone before I could get his name. But that bright and glowing countenance and those potent words shall ever linger in memory.

Deny the Adverse

"Everything once got me down," he asserted. "I was licked by practically every difficulty that came along, and believe me, they were at me constantly. Always I was expecting new and bigger difficulties and I wasn't disappointed, for they seemed to grow bigger all the time. Then," he continued, "I happened to read an article in a little magazine someone had left on a seat in a bus. It was about denying the adverse. I thought, 'How crazy can you get, that if you deny the adverse it will go away, just like that?' But the article contained a statement that made a powerful impression on me. It was this: 'If God be for us, who can be against us?'[2] As I thought about it, I personalized it: 'If God be for me, who or what can be against me?'

"Well, anyway I started denying the adverse things that were crowding me, and at the same time I practiced affirming that God was for me and what could therefore

[2]Romans 8:31.

be against me? You ought to try it," he asserted triumphantly. "It will put you on the victory road like it did me." So saying, he crushed my hand in a viselike grip and was off into the crowd.

Well, I was so impressed that I took his advice. I did start denying the adverse and affirming spiritual support and was amazed to find that the difficulties seemed fewer in number and certainly less formidable. They did not all go away, of course. In fact, I still periodically have some to deal with, and always will. But their power has lessened and my dominance over them has increased. This is a fact, a very wonderful fact.

I quoted elsewhere the statement attributed to Sigmund Freud to the effect that the chief duty of a human being is to endure life. That we must endure certain things, learn to live with some factors that are unpleasant and from which there seems to be no alternative, is, of course, true, at least in our present state of unenlightenment. But if that were the entire story, existence would be pretty grim. I prefer to think that the chief duty of a human being is to get on top of life and its difficulties. This chapter, therefore, is about the power of in-depth faith to help us win over those difficulties. The man in Canada, in our brief but unforgettable encounter, transmitted the fact of an intense belief as the source of his remarkable ability to deny the adverse. It proved to be a dynamic new expression of the positive principle.

Organize Your Difficulties

The famous research scientist Charles F. Kettering once indicated that a good statement of a problem is half the solution. One important step in handling difficulties is to organize them in orderly fashion so that you are able to see them as they actually are and each in relation to the other. Themistocles, a famed soldier-statesman of antiquity, called attention to the value of talking a problem out rather than thinking of it subjectively: "The speech of man is like embroidered tapestries, since like them this too has to be extended in order to display its patterns, but when it is rolled up it conceals and distorts them."[3] Similarly, the elements of a problem, when fear or panic are involved, tend to assume a degree of formidability not warranted by the facts. Well-organized facts are what we must have if any problem is to be successfully solved.

Another reason a practical faith is of utmost importance and value is that one of its by-products is a non-emotionalized reaction to any problem. A believer of this stature, having had the fear element reduced if not entirely eliminated, is thereby able to think clearly and with objectivity. He sees facts as they are and not as colored by emotionally tinctured supposition. He is able to face up to a situation that, if viewed emotionally, could seem extremely difficult if not impossible, and proceed to get a good outcome.

Faith too often has been made to appear as a kind of vague, churchy point of view, a sort of nice attitude, but really out of touch with hard reality. Fortunately, people today are now aware that faith is much more than that; indeed, it is a dynamic process of mind conditioned by practical and scientific formulas. Increasing numbers of persons are learning that spiritual teachings contain scientific and practical techniques which work when worked. A simple example in everyday living is that if you dislike people you are bound to get back dislike in return, and this tends to take the joy out of life. But if you love people, as spiritual law dictates, you inevitably get back love in return and thereby experience a joy that

[3] From Plutarch, *Lives*, *Themistocles*, Sec. 29.

makes you a happy person. So, don't be one of the so-called practical persons who wants to insist that faith is theoretical and impractical. How out-of-it can you get?

One of the chief marks of in-depth faith is common sense. A very astute businessman in a certain area was also an outstanding spiritual leader. He had that all-too-rare combination of spirituality and practicality that proves these two qualities as having natural affinity. I can still recall his whimsical version of St. Paul's words: "And now abideth faith, hope and love, these three; but the greatest of these is common sense."[4]

"As a Grain of Mustard Seed"

In-depth faith and its practical system of organizing the mind when dealing with difficulties were pointed up by the experience of a television interviewer when I was a guest on his popular show in a city in the Southwest. He wanted to discuss what he called my ideas of positive thinking and their relation to spiritual concepts. In the interview I outlined my positive spiritual techniques of thought and action and insisted that they were practical, viable and highly workable. I remember saying that the spiritual mind is an organized mind which has the power to handle problems with extra effectiveness because it can marshal all factors for a scientific approach to the problem.

This concept rather threw my host, as he had the traditional notion that the spiritual is some sort of idealized and dreamy attitude quite unrelated to the practical affairs of the world. "You mean to say that by this thing which you call in-depth faith I can solve a personal problem that happens to be worrying me at the present time?"

"Certainly," I responded.

[4] I Corinthians 13:13 (paraphrased).

"But," he continued, "my faith cannot, even by stretching, be called in-depth. In fact, while I do believe, still and all my faith is, you might say, rather cursory and indefinite."

I told him that he did not need to have all that much faith and quoted the words "If ye have faith as a grain of mustard seed [small but real] . . . nothing shall be impossible unto you,"[5] adding that the question isn't the extent of one's faith but the reality and in-depth quality of that which he does have. Even the essence, when it is honest and real, has the power.

How He Sold His House

Our TV conversation went on before a big crowd in the studio and of course a large listening audience over the air, and I was careful, as always, to make no claims that could not be factually substantiated. Indeed, I have never knowingly, in public talks, in books or articles, or in a one-to-one conversation made any statement that I did not believe to be absolute truth or one that could not be attested to by the experience of myself or others whose veracity I trusted. So therefore when he outlined his personal problem I assured him that by the application of scientific spiritual principles he could get a practical answer that would be right and proper for all concerned.

This man explained that he had nearly all his savings tied up in a house in a Michigan city from which he had some months previously been transferred to his present location. He had tried every possible way to sell this house, but with no result. Meanwhile, nothing was coming in from the property and he was hard hit with taxes. Finally he had tried prayer "as a last resort," but even

[5]Matthew 17:20.

this extreme expediency had not worked. He was "still stuck with the house." "Now," he said, "here you come along with this idea of in-depth faith as a practical system of procedure. Now get me straight; I really don't doubt what you say and I know you sincerely believe it to be true, but I sure would like to know how to apply these common sense precepts to my practical problem."

"Okay," I replied, "let's take a look at what you have been doing. Let us organize this problem. From the way you tell it, I get the reaction that you are pretty uptight about the matter. That must first of all be corrected, for sound, practical thinking never comes through an uptight thought system. Secondly, I get the notion that you want to make a killing on this sale. I don't blame you for wanting a fair profit, but greediness is self-defeating as a usual thing."

"You've got me on both counts," he confessed. "Maybe I have priced it higher than a fair consideration warrants."

"Now you say you have desperately turned to prayer. Desperate prayer," I pointed out, "is much less effective than affirmative prayer, in which you confidently affirm that forces are now in motion on a spiritual basis that will culminate in a satisfactory sale of the house. Relax mentally and get your mind into the unhurried tempo at which spiritual things happen," I said.

Finally I asked him about whom he was thinking in this hoped-for transaction. Surprised, he answered, "Myself. Who else?" I then went on to another principle which I felt was important. I asked him to visualize the type of people for whom the house would be ideal. He replied, "I've never thought of that. It really is just made for a young couple with three children."

"Well, then, what do you say we form a mental image of such a family, one that is searching for just that sort of house, and 'see' them as finding yours? Now, when they come to see the house, since you know that it is intended for them, work out terms that will help them to buy it and by which you can come out all right on your investment." He gave me a strange sort of look. "Do you know something? That makes sense. It really does. I'll work at it."

With astonishment but also with enthusiasm, he telephoned me a few weeks later. "They did come—just the family we visualized. And they are wonderful people. We made a deal, one that is fair to each. And, boy, am I sold on that practical and scientific in-depth faith principle!"

"Glad things worked out so splendidly." I replied, equally pleased, and then added, "Keep it going." And why not, for it is a fact, a true fact, that in-depth faith wins over all difficulties. So why be defeated by difficulties when defeat is not at all necessary, especially since you have the spiritual formula that turns defeat into success?

Power of Mental Conditioning

The human mind is an amazing instrument and the thoughts that activate it can determine what happens to a person and how well he handles the problems which come up daily. In a true sense we are what we think over a long period of time. At this moment you are what your dominant thought pattern has been, shall we say, over the past ten years or so. If you and I want to know what we will be ten years from this date, the answer can very well be in terms of what you and I think over the coming decade. The positive principle is a scientific thought process designed to make things better, ever better.

Fear thoughts can destroy creative capacity, and what is of even more sinister effect, they can bring to pass

206

things that are constantly feared. One of the most arresting statements in that book of truth called the Bible is this terrible line: "The thing which I greatly feared is come upon me. . . ."[6] By persistently fearing some trouble or illness or accident or failure, and by keeping that fear vital and active over a length of time, forces are encouraged, perhaps even created, that actualize those things so long feared.

Likewise, things that have long been believed, things like good outcomes and health and achievement and success, can also come upon us. While fear and negativism can destroy, faith and positivism can create and develop. It is therefore of extraordinary importance to practice persistently, doggedly, and assiduously dynamic faith attitudes. There is power in them. In more ways than one.

Baseball Team Turned Into Champions

One of the most readable of the old sportswriters was a man named Hugh Fullerton, who wrote a yarn in some newspaper years ago. I have forgotten the name of the paper but recall the story very well indeed. It was about a manager of a Texas team whose name was Josh O'Reilly. Mr. O'Reilly's team was not doing well that season despite the fact that he had seven .300 hitters on his squad. It seemed that every team in the league was regularly beating his men, who definitely had championship quality. But the team was in a deep and protracted slump, and no amount of criticism or threatening or cajoling could get them out of it.

It so happened that an evangelist named Reverend Schlater was holding meetings in the neighborhood. Reverend Schlater was reputed to be a spiritual healer,

[6]Job 3:25.

and, far and wide, people had great faith in him as almost a miracle worker.

One day, unable longer to endure his team's horrendous performance, Josh O'Reilly demanded of each player his two favorite bats. He put them in a wheelbarrow and went off with them. Later, just before that afternoon's game, the manager returned with the bats and explained that he had taken them to Reverend Schlater, who had blessed them. The players were astounded. They looked at their bats with reverential awe. And they became different men. That afternoon nothing could stop them as they drove in twenty-one runs. For the rest of the summer they hammered their way to a league championship. It was said that for years ballplayers would pay large sums of money for a Schlater bat.

Now with all due respect to Reverend Schlater, we must believe that no change was wrought in those wooden weapons called baseball bats. But a strange magic had been done to the minds of those believing men who wielded the bats. A reconditioning of their minds had taken place by which they were no longer wallowing in a defeatist slump but had instead become invincible and victorious.

The average person who supinely accepts and goes along with negative assumptions that lead him to defeat can radically change such a state of affairs by becoming a person of real faith, in-depth and powerful, the kind that wins over all difficulties. A reconditioning of the mind, intense enough to change attitudes, will enable any person to become powerfully inspired, and what is more, to keep that positive principle going whatever or however harsh a situation may be.

Always the "Break Records" Principle

The people who really go for in-depth faith are those who have a deep inner drive to do more, and then even more, with themselves. They are the extra-motivated individuals who are never content with present performance. They are inevitably driven by an inner and ceaseless urge to scale new heights, reach dizzier levels, break old records and set new achievement standards. In-depth faith, the positive principle and the climbing instinct are of the same piece.

I am writing this chapter while seated on a balcony of the Mont Cervin Hotel in Zermatt, Switzerland, of which my good friend, Theodore E. Seiler, is the owner. It is a sun-kissed afternoon, and from my balcony the great Matterhorn stands out sharp and clear, with its almost always present white cloud scarf trailing out against the blue sky. There is perhaps no mountain in the world equal in stern beauty and historical romance to this vast finger of stone standing solitary and aloof from the huge mountains in the Alpine range of which it is a part. Indeed, the Matterhorn has been described as more than a mountain; it is a presence, a brooding and ever-fascinating presence.

Men who have it in them to respond to high places have always wanted to climb the Matterhorn. In early years they feared to invade the home of the evil spirits who were presumed to dwell amid its crags and eminences, ready to hurl down ice and stone upon any intruder. Regardless of these ancient superstitions, efforts were made to find a way to the top; but for long years no climber succeeded in reaching the mysterious summit.

Then the famed Zermatt mountain guide Peter

Taugwalder made known his belief that the vast, inscrutable mountain could, for a fact, be climbed from the Zermatt side. So the British mountain climber Edward Whymper, then twenty-five years old, and a companion, Lord Francis Douglas, started out for this then isolated mountain hamlet of Zermatt. There they found the Reverend Charles Hudson, perhaps the best known of all mountaineers of the day, who had made the first ascent of the mighty Monte Rosa ten years earlier on August 1, 1855.

They organized a party of seven to make an assault on the hitherto impregnable Matterhorn. The imperious Whymper took charge, and the group included Lord Douglas, the Reverend Mr. Hudson, the guide Michel Croz, of Chamonix, Robert Hadow, a nineteen-year-old student and a rather inexperienced climber, and the two best Zermatt guides, Peter Taugwalder and his son. Together they made their courageous and audacious decision to try to scale The Mountain. Whymper describes the thrilling epic in his *Rambles in the Alps*. But it was scarcely a ramble, for while they did reach the top—the first men ever to stand on that elusive height—at 1:40 on the afternoon of July 14, 1865, their elation was short-lived. For on the descent Hadow, tired by the climb, slipped, knocking over Croz and dragging Hudson and Douglas down. The weak hemp rope connecting the two parties broke. Despite the superhuman efforts of Whymper and the two Taugwalders, the four men plunged down the four-thousand-foot terrible north wall to their deaths. For over one hundred years their skeletons have reposed somewhere in the mountain vastness. That pathetic broken rope may be seen today in the Alpine Museum in Zermatt.

Studying the Matterhorn this day, I'm impressed by a curious fact about firsts or record-breakings. Almost as soon as some person becomes the first to achieve a long-frustrated goal and breaks a record, along comes another to perform the same feat or even go beyond it. In the case of the Matterhorn's first climbing by Whymper and his companions, three days later a famed mountaineer, J. A. Carrel, and his party reached the summit on the perilous Italian side from Breuil. The glory of the first climbers was not all theirs for long, which brings to mind some thoughtful words ascribed to Goethe: "The deed is all, the glory naught."

Since those heroic men led the way, many persons have climbed the great Matterhorn. Once it was demonstrated that it could be done, others proceeded to do it also, for they were persuaded, by the example of the pioneers, to have the belief that they, too, could climb, achieve, surmount. So indeed it is the deed that is important and not the glory.

People Still Want to Climb

Times change, but do people change all that much? The motivating upthrust to get to the top is still built into people. One hundred years to the day after the first ascent of the Matterhorn, my wife and I were sitting on the terrace at Schwarzsee looking up at the little hut situated high on the flank of the mountain, from which ascents are begun at daybreak. A young man dressed for climbing came along and sat down near us. Recognizing us, he began to talk somewhat self-consciously about himself. He took a rather dim view of himself as a failure who just couldn't seem to make it. "I want to do things, accomplish something. I want to make a success in life, but at each try I seem to get knocked down," he said glumly. He told us he had been in Switzerland since early springtime, climbing hills at first, then small mountains, then bigger ones, and now he was going to take a shot at the biggest of all—the Matterhorn.

The boy seemed loath to leave, though the afternoon was waning and he was scheduled to meet his guide at the hut at sunset to be ready for the start upward at dawn. "I really believe I can do it," he mused. "I've got to do it. I've just got to climb, for if I can do this ascent I know I can move up in other things, too!" He stood up, shook hands with us and waved acknowledgment of our "Good luck—God bless you." He proceeded perhaps a hundred yards or so, then turned and came back to where we sat. With some embarrassment he asked, "Will you do me a favor?"

"Sure will; anything you ask."

"Okay, then pray for me, will you? If I can get some of that positive faith you write about, I know I can do things." So saying, he moved off up the long trek to the mountain. We watched until he disappeared around a shoulder. He did climb the Matterhorn, and has been successfully climbing other kinds of mountains ever since.

People still want to climb and break records and they are doing that regularly. Everywhere one sees the results of the in-depth faith that makes achievement possible. Everywhere are those inspired, enthusiastic and highly motivated individuals who have the spirit, the indomitable spirit, to keep the positive principle going.

The phenomenon of firsts and record-breaking as a demonstration of the extra-real faith that wins over difficulties is today occupying not a little space in newspapers. For instance, there is the story of John Walker, the New Zealand mile runner, who ran the mile in 3 minutes 49.4 seconds, slicing 1.6 seconds off the previous record of 3:51 set by Filbert Bayi of Tanzania. Walker was the first runner ever to go the mile distance in less than 3 minutes 51 seconds.

All this brings back memories of the era when sports writers were of the unanimous opinion that it was impossible for anyone to run the mile in four minutes flat, and that it would never be done. Well, "never" is a long time and he is foolish indeed who believes that it can "never" be done by anyone. Mile runners' sights continued to be fixed on that "impossible" four-minute mark. Sweden's famous Gunder Haegg and Arne Andersson both got near to it, but the man who made track history was Britain's Roger Bannister, who achieved this proclaimed "impossible" in 1954 at Oxford by clocking the mile at 3:59.4.

To the objection that big-time mountain climbing and mile running have no bearing on the average individual, the fact is that the principle of climbing and breaking past records is applicable to all activity. To be more than you are, to do more than you are doing, to achieve higher standards and greater results are definitely inherent in each of us. And constantly persons like the readers of this book are aiming for and achieving higher and ever higher marks in whatever their goals may be. The principle of in-depth faith is of powerful help in keeping the motivation going, even in the presence of setbacks.

My longtime friend Frank Wangeman, vice-president and general manager of the Waldorf-Astoria Hotel in New York City, in commenting upon setbacks, made a wise and pertinent remark: "Maturity of experience," he declared, "proves that no setback is final." With in-depth faith one can just keep going, regardless of resistance, until finally all difficulties are overcome. And then with whetted anticipation of more victories, you are ready to take on a new flock of setbacks and so break ever new records, continuing in this valiant manner throughout life on the basis of the positive principle.

Perhaps one of the chief and most desirable qualities

of all is to have the ability to persevere doggedly against adverse conditions. In a review of a book called *Nothing Venture, Nothing Win*, by Sir Edmund Hillary, famous climber of Mount Everest, the reviewer, John Rupp, pictures Hillary as "a formidable man." "When he and his party were attempting to move up-river through appalling rapids, Hillary says, 'at any moment we felt we must come to easier water and we became so engrossed in the struggle that the dangers were forgotten.' " What a stimulating thought! Engrossed in the struggle, Hillary was able to overcome his fears. So, the prime secret is to hang in there and always keep going.

The late, great, big-league baseball manager Casey Stengel had it right. It was said of him, "Defeat did not awe Casey, for he was on good terms with hope. In the midst of defeat he was always looking for victory." Which, of course, was one reason his victory average was very high indeed.

He Reprogrammed His Thinking

In the title of this chapter we have made a rather all-inclusive claim in the statement that in-depth faith wins over all difficulties. This might be modified by the semi-doubting person to an acknowledgment that one can win over some, perhaps even over many, difficulties, but to be all-inclusive is a strain on credulity. But having observed the amazing power of in-depth belief, I long since came to the conclusion that the power of down-deep and all-out faith is infinitely greater than the average person estimates. In my experience, both personally and from observation of others who live out a wholly committed faith in God, it is definitely possible to live with, adjust to, or win over all difficulties, without qualification.

I was scheduled to speak to a public meeting of busi-

ness people in an eastern city and upon arrival at the
hall entered by the stage door and took a seat backstage
while waiting for the program to begin. Soon a rather
stocky, well-built man of above-average height came
back to where I waited and introduced himself as the
master of ceremonies for the meeting. He was an ani-
mated person, obviously charged with vigor and enthusiasm, and I was impressed by his positive spirit and
attitude.

He told me that he had been a helicopter pilot in the
war in Southeast Asia. He was shot down, and in such
serious physical condition that it was expected he would
die. Due to suspected brain damage, doctors came to a
projected diagnosis that if he did live he would, as he
expressed it, "be a vegetable." Indeed, he did undergo a
brain operation, and parted his hair to indicate a plate
in the top of the head. Removed to a military hospital in
the United States, he was unable to move his legs or
arms. But speech was not affected, nor was his ability to
think.

One day he said to his wife, "I want you to bring me a
book I once read by Norman Vincent Peale and read it
to me." Day after day his wife read about the powerful
creative and re-creative principles of faith and positive
thinking until this desperately wounded man developed
an intensity of faith in God's healing power, as well as in
his own power of self re-creation. Then came the conviction that he, too, could be healed despite the dis-
heartening prognosis.

He told his wife that, beginning then, he was going to
reprogram his mind. He would work with the power of
the mind to take charge of his broken body through an
in-depth faith in God and in himself. Accordingly, he
entered upon an intensive and persistent routine of belief and faith plus spiritual affirmation, thus infusing his

mind with a powerful directive force. The healing did not come in a miraculous manner nor all that easily, but it did come, as was evidenced by the physically strong and mentally alert person who told me this story. It is an example of what a motivated human being can do with himself when his faith is strong and deep enough in content and force. Later as I watched this remarkable man emcee the meeting with humor and spirit that set a tone positive and enthusiastic in nature, I once again reaffirmed my own certain belief that in-depth faith does, for a great, big, glorious fact, win over all difficulties. So keep the positive principle going—always keep it going.

Finally, let us recapitulate in brief the ideas and principles put forward in this chapter:

1. Seek until you get a certainty of The Presence. Then, like Jerry Adams, you will be afraid no more.
2. Know for a fact that you are never alone. A great Someone is with you always.
3. Believe that you are bigger than your difficulties, for you are, indeed.
4. Through study and practice, develop intensity of belief, in-depth faith, as contrasted with the nominal variety.
5. Become expert in denying the adverse.
6. Organize your difficulties and problems. Then you will have half the solution, and the rest will come more surely and easily.
7. Learn the relationship between in-depth faith and common sense.
8. Practice until you develop expertise in the power of mental conditioning.
9. Always keep going the "break records" principle.
10. Retain the vital "want to climb" instinct that has been built into you.
11. Reprogram your thinking and become an indepth practitioner of the positive principle. Then miracles will start happening.

TWELFTH
WAY TO KEEP
THE POSITIVE
PRINCIPLE GOING

Keep Going Strong With the Excitement Principle

The night was bitter cold—30 degrees below zero. Some 18,000 United States Marines in Korea were facing nearly 100,000 Communist troops. And both sides expected battle in the morning. Now, at midnight, a huge marine was standing by a tank, its metal sides so intensely cold that fingers actually stuck to it. Blue with cold, covered with caked and frozen mud, tiny icicles hanging from his heavy beard, the marine was eating cold beans out of a can with a penknife.

A newspaper correspondent watched the big marine as he ate his unappetizing meal, leaning against the tank in a bleak climate and facing an uncertain future. Evidently the newsman was impelled to some philosophical thinking, for suddenly he put to the marine a profound question: "If I were God," he asked, "and were able to give you anything, what would you ask for?"

The marine, continuing to eat his cold beans, reflected long before answering; but when he did speak, his statement was equal in philosophical content to the question. The simple reply was "I would ask for tomorrow."

This man, in a dismal and critical situation, ready to do whatever circumstances might demand of him, had one desire; and that desire was for continuing life, a tomorrow with home and family and a future.

Since the desire for vital life is basic in the consciousness of every person, it is natural to respond to motivation, to inspiration, to enthusiasm, to dynamic stimuli, all of which give reality and meaning to the experience of living.

Having written a number of books and given many speeches on inspirational subjects, I have had some experience in judging human response to the power of motivational thinking. People generally want to be inspired and they respond to enthusiasm when they relinquish desultory and negative attitudes. When so released, most men and women eagerly go for a vital quality of positive thought and action like the excitement principle. As a result, many become genuinely inspired and enthusiastic and thereby move to an upper level of living, one that is superior to anything previously experienced.

To Keep the Positive Principle Going Requires Skill

But to maintain a high level of enthusiasm and inspiration and to keep it going constantly over a long period of time is not all that easy. It requires consistent reinspiration, renewed motivation, together with education in the skills of controlling and directing mental processes. Motivational attitudes are subjected daily to a terrific bombardment of depressed, gloomy and negative ideas. It seems that there is, in effect at least, though probably not in any sense planned, what amounts to an effort to undermine positive and hopeful attitudes about the country, about the future, indeed about just everything. Some years ago there was a radio news commentator in the New York area who came on the air many a night with the gloomy words "There's bad news tonight, folks." While current news commentators do not perhaps use that particular trademark, to some extent they are professional purveyors of bad news, professional under-miners of positive thinking.

Of course there is bad news, indeed quite a lot of it, but of late years it has been so constantly underscored that the casual listener or reader comes to assume that there is no good news at all, that the country and the world and even life itself are just one gigantic flop. One wonders why, along with the bad news, there cannot be some such creative emphasis as, for example, "There's bad news tonight, folks, but so what? We've got what it takes to improve things." That might go far toward changing the bad news into good news.

Actually, I do not intend to be critical. My purpose is constructive in simply raising the question as to why we cannot be equally concerned with positive solutions as with negatives. As a onetime newspaper reporter, I am aware that news is a departure from the normal state of affairs. As the old saying had it, "When a dog bites a boy, that is not news, because it happens so often. But if a boy bites a dog, that is news."[1] If the time should ever arrive when it becomes news to report decent, law-abiding people, instead of chronicling the actions of thieves and criminals, we would indeed be in a sorry mess. The good is still the norm, and departure from the good is still news.

But the individual who desires to move to an upper level of motivation and enthusiasm must maintain a discriminating thought skill: namely, the ability to deal with the negative creatively but at the same time to reject the assumption that he must become a negative thinker to be an "in" person.

Enthusiasm and positive attitudes being under constant bombardment from negative and depressive sources, the individual who wants to be an upbeat type

[1]John B. Boger, city editor, New York *Sun*, 1873-90.

of person is hard put to it to sustain enthusiasm. This fact, added to the ordinary run of difficulty, adversity, hardship, sickness, sorrow and trouble, can take an extraordinary toll of one's inspirational vigor. It is to counteract this siphoning off of inspiration that I have written this book, *The Positive Principle Today.* The purpose throughout the book has been to suggest ways and means, workable procedures for keeping inspiration, motivation and enthusiasm going in the face of the attacks upon this positive pattern of thought and action by the adverse, the difficult, the negative.

Maintain Buildup of Spirit

To keep it going requires a vigorous counterattack against the erosion of inspirational attitudes, and this consists, we believe, of a buildup of spirit. The word "inspiration" actually means an enspiriting or renewable infusion of fresh and powerful new spirit-vitality. Since spirit under constant blows tends to run down, we must become so organized mentally that almost automatically, instead of running down, spirit runs up again. The creative factor involved in this process is a constant repowering of the thought pattern, undeviating emphasis upon the excitement principle.

I am reminded of an old lady whom my wife and I recently encountered on a fairly rugged mountain trail at Rifflealp near the Gornergrat in Switzerland. On these trails devotees of high-altitude hiking have a sort of camaraderie and, it being the German-speaking part of Switzerland, the usual greeting is *"Gruss Gott,"* or "Greeting in God's name." This elderly lady was hunched over and walking with the aid of a sturdy cane in a kind of dogged determination. She was accompanied by a man, obviously a guide. As we met she looked up at us with bright eyes from under an old-fashioned hat. Instead of the previously mentioned usual greeting, she said, *"Bonjour, madame, bonjour, monsieur."*

"Bonjour, madame," we replied. Whereupon she went into a rapid flurry of French, to which finally I said, *"Ah, madame, non parle français."* At which she veered into Italian and then into German, and while I can struggle through a simple conversation in the latter language, she saw that she was not communicating too well.

"You look like an American; perhaps you can speak English," she laughed merrily.

"Yes, madam, I talk some English, American style."

"Oh, I like American style," she said, "it's so picturesque."

She then informed us that she was eighty-nine years old. "You are a wonderful woman," I commented admiringly. "You speak four languages fluently, your mind is sharp, you wear no glasses and you climb mountain trails at age eighty-nine. Just how do you keep going so strongly?"

"Oh," she replied, "you see, I'm so excited about everything. The world is such a wonderful place; people are so interesting. In fact, I awaken every morning with as much excitement as when I was a girl."

"Well," I said, "if you were as excited then as you are now at eighty-nine, you must have been a ball of fire when you were young."

"But you see, monsieur, I am still young. Oh, yes, this body is a bit warped in the back, but I'm quite strong and healthy. But it is the spirit that makes the difference. I'm excited because my spirit lives in a perpetual state of excitement."

"You mean that you keep it going with the excitement principle?"

With a bright smile she answered, "Oui, oui, monsieur, that is it precisely. I keep it going with—what do you call it?—the excitement principle. That is good —really good—the excitement principle." So saying, she moved away, on up the trail, pushing resolutely ahead with her cane against a backdrop of mighty peaks. We watched her, marveling at how tremendous a human being can be when the spirit remains strong, even invulnerable. No matter the onslaughts of depressives and adversities, such a person can always keep going and going strong with that precious secret of spirit buildup, the excitement principle.

Practice Being Excited

The acquiring of skill in mental attitudes, as in all aspects of perfection, requires practice. One can hardly expect to keep excitement going unless one practices being excited. And a viable method of practice is deliberately to think in terms of how exciting life is, how exciting your job, how fascinating your opportunities. I once knew an actress in the movies, a brilliant artist, a woman named Hattie McDaniel. She was a rare and radiant personality. She told me that it was her custom to step outside every morning and no matter what the weather conditions, rain or sunshine, she would say aloud, "Hello there, good morning! You're so wonderful; I'm so terribly excited to be alive. Thanks, dear God—thanks a lot!" Hattie McDaniel practiced the excitement principle and so became an exciting and unforgettable person.

Everywhere I meet these exciting people who are practicing the excitement principle. I was breakfasting one morning with a man in a Los Angeles hotel. The coffee shop had a beautiful canary-color motif. Our waitress wore a nice outfit of similar hue. But it was the girl's spirit that captivated us. "Good morning, gentlemen. Now for a delicious breakfast that will set you up for a wonderful day. Everything we have is good. Let me bring you something nice." Actually she didn't even take an order, and we were so impressed that we thought the food she set before us was perfect. As we left the restaurant she said, "Think a good day and have a good day."

"Where did you get that terrific thought?" I asked.

"Why, from you," she answered brightly. "One of your 'Pocket' cards—'Think a good day, plan a good day, pray a good day.'"

"Well," I commented, "you certainly have improved on my writing."

"Oh, you see, I find that if you practice being excited, that is the way it is."

The practice of excitement can bring anyone out of the doldrums of downbeat thinking. For example, I received a telephone call from a jeweler in a southern city who was very depressed and discouraged. He said he was a reader of my books and, while he at times thought he had got the hang of the positive principle, still he could not stick with it. How could he keep it going, especially when he was in such a dull business as selling jewelry, a business bequeathed by his father?

I expressed astonishment that he could possibly appraise a jewelry business as a dull occupation, pointing out the romance inherent in diamonds and other gems and that jewelry is related to the instinct for beauty and is symbolic of love and affection. Indeed, I argued, any commodity for the welfare of people, even bread and sugar and vegetables, could not be construed as dull, for they are of the essence of life. And jewelry, relating as it does to the expression of thoughts too deep for words, should be perpetually exciting.

"But," he complained, "economic conditions in our

area are not very good and people are not buying luxury items under these circumstances."

I even questioned the rationale of writing off his merchandise as a luxury item to be marketable only in affluent times. "Beauty," I countered, "is a necessity of the human spirit, especially when it speaks of romance and abiding affection. And that is even more important when times are hard."

I asked him to read me samples of his local advertising. One ad read, "Buy Jewelry at X's, Oldest Quality Merchants in the County.' And another: "Finest Jewelry at X's, Founded 1893." "Well," I said, "I am no expert in advertising copywriting, but I think you are only stating the obvious—that you have been in business a long while and are dealers in quality merchandise. That is true, of course, but hardly likely to motivate the buyer. He or she must be reached emotionally if desirable action is to be stimulated."

"Okay," he responded, "what would you suggest?"

Hardly taking his request seriously, I said, "Well, how about this? 'Put a sparkle on her finger like the sparkle in her eye.' That is for the young and in love. Another might be, 'A wedding ring from X's will be just as beautiful when there are silver threads among the gold.' And how about this for an aged woman on an anniversary: 'Add the beauty of her toil-worn hands to the loveliness of a ring from X's famous jewelry shop.' " And so on.

"Boy," he said, "come down here and I will give you a job. You almost make me want to buy my own things."

"I want to bring some excitement into you about the wonderful opportunity you have of putting lights in people's eyes and smiles on their faces by your articles of beauty. Tell you what. Every morning when you awaken, say aloud, 'How exciting to be a dealer in jewelry! All day long I'm going to bring that extra touch of joy to young and old.' Practice enthusiasm and excitement and, as you do, inspiration will come flooding back into your mind. Then keep it going."

This is the procedure that really keeps it going. Think excitement, talk excitement, act out excitement, and you are bound to become an excited person. Life will take on new zest, deeper interest and greater meaning. You can think, talk and act yourself into dullness or into monotony or into unhappiness. By the same process you can build up inspiration, excitement and a surging depth of joy. For a fact, we tend to become precisely what we practice, whether gloominess or excitement. And, since the latter is so much more to be desired, the part of wisdom is to keep it going by the daily practice of the excitement principle.

Super-Salesman From Sorrento

I have great admiration and pride in the career of a positive and energetic young man, John Milano, whom I first met nearly twenty years ago in Sorrento, Italy. While visiting that beautiful town Mrs. Peale and I went into a shop where we were greeted by an attractive, friendly and, I must say, persuasive young man who spoke excellent English.

He proceeded to show Mrs. Peale his merchandise and, because I recognize a master salesman when I see one in operation, I at once became aware of the impending danger to my pocketbook. And indeed he did sell my wife a rather large order. Watching the young man operate, I admired the force and charm of his personality, recognizing at once the outstanding ability which he so obviously possessed.

I asked John about his aspirations and goals and he replied that he wanted to go to America and be an American businessman working in the opportunity afforded by the American system of free enterprise. He waxed quite enthusiastic as he outlined his clearly defined objectives. But then he added that it was difficult to get to America, having little money and no one to help him.

Becoming more interested in this dynamic individual, I outlined the principles of visualization, explaining that a specific goal held tenaciously in mind will develop in consciousness into actuality. I suggested that he study and practice the power of positive thinking, meanwhile affirming and re-affirming that he would achieve his specified ambition of becoming an American businessman. Then I added, because I became enthusiastic, that when he came to New York he was to look me up and I would help him secure a job. This was, you might say, going out on a limb; but my enthusiasm was unbounded.

Sure enough, in a few months John showed up in my New York office to get the promised job. It was getting along toward Christmas and I wrote to presidents of a half dozen of the leading men's shops in the city somewhat as follows and listing on each letter the various store executives to whom the same letter was going:

Dear Sir:
    In Sorrento, Italy, I met the greatest natural-born salesman I have ever encountered, and my acquaintance with super-salesmen is considerable. This man is now in New York and is available for a position. The first one of you who responds to this letter gets him.

Sincerely yours,

The response was immediate, and John was assigned to the men's hat department of a Fifth Avenue haberdashery. When the Christmas business season ended, special help was let go; but not John, whose selling ability was recognized. And so the years passed until only recently I received a letter from John Milano, now president of possibly the largest hat manufacturing company in the country. And when I dress up, whose hat do you think I am wearing? Why, of course, it is a beautiful hat of which I'm very proud, a gift from my old friend, the super-salesman of Sorrento, now one of America's successful businessmen.

In the light of such a human story who can say that America is no longer the land of opportunity? It is, and always will be for the positive-thinking, motivated and excited John Milanos. They are the men who live by the positive principle and know how to keep it going. In so doing they keep America going.

Get Interested, Intensely Interested

Interested people are excited people. In such persons the zest for living does not run down. They keep the fun of work and responsibility and the fascination of involvement always going, and that in turn keeps them going. Others may run down in spirit and grow into the "I've had it" type, but this never happens to the intensely interested.

On a speaking trip I encountered Senator Everett Dirksen in one of the long walkways of O'Hare Airport in Chicago. I had met him before and, indeed, had once spoken with him on the same platform at a trade association convention, but that had been several years previously and I was not at all sure he would remember me. So I started to introduce myself. "My name is—"

"Now, hold it," he said, taking my hand in both of his. "Norman Vincent Peale. Do you recall that night when we spoke together? And here is what you said in your speech." To my utter astonishment, he repeated my remarks almost word for word. Indeed, with his remarkable gift for speech he enhanced them considerably.

"How," I asked, "can you, with all your activity, remember so accurately an occasion several years past and so amazingly repeat a talk made by a fellow speaker?"

"The reason, Norman," he replied, "is that I was interested. I'm always interested. Every experience becomes vivid for me and indelibly imprinted on my mind because I am interested." Then he went on in his inimitable way to talk about the fascination, the excitement of public speaking on subjects of importance to human well-being. The senator has now gone on, but never shall I forget those moments when I listened to him in that busy airport as he poured out the zest and unalloyed excitement of his facile mind. Everett Dirksen surely ranks among the few greatest public speakers in American history, an exciting, dynamic speaker, and the secret was his eager and profound interest in people and in affairs.

Once, in the old Cleveland railroad station early one morning, I ran into my longtime friend, former Congressman Walter Judd, and we had breakfast together at the lunch counter. He told me of the number of speeches he was making that week all over the country, and I commented on how tired he must be and didn't such a program take it out of him? "Not at all, not at all," he replied energetically. "You see, I believe in everything I say and am intensely interested, so how can I run down?" Here was a great and perpetually excited man. Both of these men practiced the excitement principle and so they knew how to keep going in high gear.

Exciting Change of Life-Style

Some years ago, an attractive and very chic young woman made an appointment to see me at my office in

Marble Collegiate Church. Her name was Mary Brinig and she had, it appeared, two objects in mind. One was to tell about how her life had been changed spiritually. She spoke in a sincere, charming and most affecting manner. She explained that she and her husband, Harold, a paper manufacturer's representative, had both found an exciting new life pattern which had brought amazing joy and meaning to them and had a powerful compulsion to share it with other people who were perhaps still going down dead-end roads.

Mary Brinig's other purpose in calling on me was to offer their services in establishing creative spiritual relationships with people who were not so fortunate as themselves in finding answers to the problems of modern living. I soon became impressed with the outgoing and profound interest of Harold and Mary in the younger people with whom New York City is filled who, for one reason or another, had missed the secret of satisfying and constructive living. I soon saw that they had a rare skill in getting to know such people and in establishing a communicable relationship with them. Having found their own answers by committing their lives to God, the manner in which they transmitted this experience to the most diverse and unexpected types of individuals marked them as two of the most effective people I have ever known or known about.

The secret of this couple is a combination of profound commitment, a love of people and a consuming interest in helping them. They brought to an exciting life-style some of the most desperately defeated. Always excited, always loving, as well as being down-to-earth and intelligent, they attracted to themselves and, through them, to God hundreds of people over the years who also found new and exciting life.

Finally Harold and Mary left New York to live in a small village in New Hampshire. There they found the same modern people-problems as in New York. Recently Ruth and I visited them and sat with a group of attractive moderns who had also found that effervescent excitement which, of all motivational forces, possesses the power to keep life going strong. The Brinigs, from a depth of spiritual reality, became practitioners of the excitement principle. And the outgoing quality of their interest in people helped them to find true happiness and kept them perpetually charged with excitement and youthfulness.

Excited and interested people are to be found in all lines of activity. And such people never have a dull job, because they are not themselves dull. At long last, life is inevitably what you are. If you are prosaic and apathetic, your job and indeed your life will reveal those same characteristics. But when you experience a spiritual awakening and come alive in the mind and in the spirit, then that old dull job becomes invested with excitement . . . even, you might say, with glory.

"All Heaven Broke Loose"

On the highway when I see a lot of trucks parked at an eating place I always stop for a meal, for these men know where the good food is. One night I sat at a counter beside a long-haul truck driver and soon we were having a sprightly conversation; couldn't help it, for this man was full of fun and laughter. And when I introduced myself, this big jovial fellow seemed to know me.

He told me, "Over many years I have seen about as much concrete as any man alive. Day after day, night after night, it was always the same, rolling down interminable miles of concrete or blacktop. The monotony of it, the absence from home, the lousy motels, the go, go, go of it, made me hate it. What a dull, drab, no-account life. I detested it.

"Then," he continued, "our boss subscribed for your magazine, *Guideposts*, for all of his employees. And I got to taking it with me to read on trips. Those stories of how people found happiness and excited living through getting close to God finally began getting to me. I had never prayed much, except when in trouble. God was just a name, actually, I'm ashamed to say, more of a swearword than anything.

"But one night I was rolling down the Ohio Turnpike and for no reason at all I began talking to God just like He was riding with me in the cab. I opened my heart and told Him everything. And I had the feeling He was right there listening, I really did, for a fact.

"Then suddenly 'all heaven broke loose'—I was happier than ever in my life. I began to cry and then to sing. I bellowed out hymns I'd learned long ago in Sunday School but thought I had forgotten. Don't know whatever in the world happened to me, but suddenly I was an altogether different man. And I've been happy ever since, and I mean happy. I love this job now, for God rolls with me every mile, every night, every day, all the way."

Talk about being excited! This man gave me a terrific lift, one that has stayed with me ever since. He was the living embodiment of the excitement principle. I stood watching in admiration as his huge truck roared off into the night. And I kept repeating that vibrant phrase of his: "all heaven broke loose." As I drove down the road in the opposite direction, I recalled some delightful lines by a good friend, J. Sig Paulson, who said:

> Sometimes I throb with laughter
> and tingle with glee

> As I ponder
> the delightful, inevitable
> project of being me!

That is the excitement principle in action, and the positive principle too!

The Fascination and the Thrill

In Chapter 4 I spoke about the importance of maintaining enthusiasm in old age. Certainly practicing the excitement principle is equally vital no matter what one's age. You can keep your life going with vitality as long as the mind and the spirit are alive and zestful. There is no logical reason why the life force should be inhibited or permitted to decline unless, of course, some devastating physical disability occurs. But even in such cases many persons have been able to keep the positive principle operative by a strong dominance of the mind and the spirit over the physical.

How pathetic is the unhealthy preoccupation of Americans with age. At the very outset of hiring, at perhaps age twenty, retirement and pensions and the end of the road are built into the work psychology. Then it is "ten years until retirement"; "only five years to go, then I'm on the shelf." So goes the mournful tune. To anyone who has added up a few years comes the warning-tinctured advice: "You would do well to ease it off. Better slow down. Remember, you're not as young as you once were." How many times have well-meaning friends come up with these cautionary and negatively tinged remarks.

Personally, this author has never entertained any thought of retiring or of slowing down. Of course, I may reshuffle the several different types of work which have consumed my time for years; but as for quitting, that is inconceivable. I have never found work to be a hardship or a chore; certainly never a bore. It is truly enjoyable, even exciting. I intend to keep on being interested, active, excited and, as they say "with it"—always with it. No ease-up, no slowdown; but, rather, to give it all I've got every day all the way.

When one job ends for any reason, find another, even in a different area or field of endeavor. Some of the happiest years for many have been those spent in activity unrelated to their life work pattern. Only this will satisfy creative desire and keep happiness going at top level. Why quit? The total life-span seems almost too short as it is.

House Packed; Mostly Young People

There are many great human beings who have the same viewpoint of forgetting age and continuously living on the positive vitality principle. Recently in London Ruth and I attended a performance by Dame Edith Evans at the Haymarket Theatre. She was appearing in *An Evening of Entertainment*. The program notes showed that Dame Edith's career began about 1912.

The house was packed to the third balcony and, surprisingly, the audience had a high percentage of young people. The curtain went up on an empty stage. Movie clips of Dame Edith's long career appeared on a screen. Then came on this white-haired woman who had to be well over eighty years of age. Her hands, I noted, though graceful, had a parchment-like look. Dressed in a white gown, she came forward with an ever-so-slight totter.

She proceeded to give readings ranging all the way from Amy Lowell of New England to William Shakespeare of Stratford-on-Avon. And they were read, too, every word of them. At times she would fumble her glasses down toward the end of her nose, perhaps to see her manuscript a little better; and there was a bit of quaver in her voice.

Alone on a vast stage! I, myself, not in the same league with her, have had to walk out before big audiences on a stage all by myself and, believe me, that is not an easy thing to do. But Dame Edith was perfectly poised and, in a charming though not strong voice, performed masterfully. I sat marveling. What did she have that enabled her to grip these people so powerfully? And the young people were shouting "Bravo!" to a woman old enough to be great-grandmother to some. She was calm; she was self-assured, because she knew from years of experience how to draw an audience to herself. Her secret was, in part at least, that she simply forgot her age and lived her life. She was just going on being the great person she had always been. She was perpetually interested, perennially excited, constantly thrilled.

Sometimes the tendency of older people (to say nothing of younger ones) is to get into the habit of thinking negatively about so many things that living loses its flavor. Life gets dull because the individual gets dull. I once advised such a man to try a simple formula designed to put the zest back into living. Every morning, first thing, he was to say aloud three times, "What do you know—life is terrific!"—the first part of the sentence an affirmation of surprise, the second an affirmation of its quality. Sure—that practice could be written off as superficial. But what do you know—it worked! That man took on new interest. He came alive.

A friend, an insurance executive, was coming up to retirement due to age. His spirit was aging, too, for he could think of nothing else. Then he had a vital spiritual experience and astonished everyone, including himself, by the amazing manner in which he rebounded right back into the marked excitement that had characterized him in earlier years.

When he retired he moved to a small upstate village and got into all sorts of activity. He found two cronies, retired men like himself—one an engineer, the other an accountant. All three were handy with tools and could do anything with their hands that they put their minds to. When one found a job to be done, the other two pitched in to help do the work. All three were active in church and community affairs. Together, in one project, they transformed an old barn on the church property into an educational and recreational building, utilizing the horse stalls as classrooms. The low haymow was made into a stage for dramatics. When my friend stopped by my house recently, I invited him to stay the night. "Thanks," he said, "I'd love to, but I can't. Got to get home for a project we are starting tomorrow morning." And with that he was off, radiating vigor, happiness, interest. According to his reports, "Everything is terrific. My only complaint is that I run out of time." He is certainly keeping it going with the excitement principle.

Think Future

The positive principle never thinks in past terms but always thinks future. "The best is yet to be" is its poetic expression. Such a positive-principle thinker is an older man who wrote to say that he had read a book of mine with good results. In fact, he was very excited about it. He explained that he had endured an inferiority complex from childhood and was now ninety-three years of age. This was by all counts the longest inferiority complex I had ever known about. "I read your book on positive thinking. I studied it. I believed it. I practiced it and am now writing to give you the good news that after ninety-three years I am at last free of my inferiority complex." But the payoff was in the P.S.: "The future looks great!"

Everywhere today one hears a dismal phrase from old and young alike: "I've had it." This variously expresses boredom or weariness. It also means, "I'm a 'through' person. My future is behind me. There's nothing ahead." But the future thinker has never "had it." Always out there ahead is the great excitement, the big thrill, the wonderful goal.

I well recall the day when the famed baseball executive Branch Rickey had been fifty years a leader in big-league baseball. Rickey, whom many authorities consider one of the greatest men the sport ever produced, was a strong, vigorous, dynamic person until almost the moment of his death at age eighty-three. He was invariably excited and enthusiastic. On his fiftieth anniversary he was asked, "What was your greatest experience in fifty years of baseball?"

Rickey drew down his bushy eyebrows and barked, "Don't know. Haven't had it yet!" Even then he was deep in plans for the formation of another big league. Branch Rickey was never an old man because he was an enthusiastic, excited, future thinker. He invariably kept the positive principle going.

Dr. Harry George Thomas, father of my friend and neighbor Lowell Thomas, possessed the same dynamic qualities which are so well demonstrated by his world-famous and adventurous son. At eighty-two Dr. Thomas enrolled as a student in a university. He did so well in his studies that he was asked to be an instructor, a faculty member, and served in this capacity until university authorities discovered that Dr. (of medicine) Thomas was eighty-four years old, nineteen years beyond retirement age! Dr. Thomas was, of course, a future thinker, practicing the power of the positive principle in so-called retirement. And currently his son, Lowell, at age eighty-four, still continues as America's oldest newscaster and is always embarking upon enthusiastic new ventures. The Thomases, it seems, are future thinkers.

Live Your Life and Forget Your Age

This type of person bases his activity on the vital principle of "Live your life and forget your age." He does not get hung up on age thoughts. Indeed, he does not think age, he does not act age, he does not talk age. As far as his mental attitude is concerned, he is ageless. His mental equipment functions in the now; always he is a "now" person. He takes himself as he is and goes on participating, doing what he has always done or something different; but still doing what he wants to do, with no concern at all about the date on his birth certificate. Or any other negative factor.

Frank Bering was still running three big hotels in Chicago—the Sherman, the Ambassador East and the Ambassador West—when well over eighty. I had known Mr. Bering since childhood. He and my mother were high school classmates in Lynchburg, Ohio.

I always stayed with Frank at the Sherman when in Chicago. One day I was speaking there at a trade association convention in the huge ballroom of the hotel. Frank was on top of everything, calm, efficient, authoritative—complete master of all the complex functioning of a 2,200-room hotel and a large convention besides.

Admiringly I said, "Frank, you sure are a great manager and executive," then asked, "How old are you?"

"What's the matter," he said, "don't you like your room? Isn't the service in this hotel okay?"

"Oh, certainly," I replied, "it's all perfect; but to think—at your age. Anyway, I know how old you are, for you were in school with my mother."

"Well, then," he said factually, "why bring it up? What has it got to do with anything as long as we are doing the job as well as or better than any half-baked forty-year-old could do it?" Then he leveled his finger at me. "Young man," he said, "I'll give you a valid principle to live by—live your life and forget your age." This man always operated on the positive principle.

Please do not get the impression that I am not fully aware of the pain and sorrow of human existence, nor that the resistances to excitement and positive attitudes are many and often severe. I have not been dealing intimately with people for a good many years without knowing that life is indeed no bed of roses. But still it is my belief that by the exercise of the positive principle we can rise above, live with and overcome the trials and problems we must face.

When recently the wife of a friend died he was, of course, devastated, but I was impressed by the depth and quality of his mental victory over his great loss and sorrow. He told me that shortly after his wife's passing he "felt" her presence most definitely and "by an inner ear" heard her speak to him. He thanked her for coming to comfort him and plaintively said, "Please come to me soon again." To which she answered, "Why, I am always near to you." Asked how he felt about the reality of this experience, he answered simply, "I'm excited to realize that she lives. She is not dead but alive. Isn't that wonderful?"

Faith of such quality is possible to those who practice the positive principle—and keep it going.

Now to add up the ideas in this chapter:

1. Keep wide open and acute your response capacity to inspiration, motivation and enthusiasm.
2. Maintain sensitivity at high level—sharp and keen.
3. Follow a steady program of renewing and revitalizing your positive attitudes. Never allow your reactions to become dull or insipid. Keep them new, fresh, vital.
4. Develop strong mental shields to ward off the bombardment of negatives.
5. Maintain a constant spirit buildup by a counterattack against the erosion of inspiration.
6. Become intensely interested. Fan your interest daily. Keep it vitalized.
7. Get the spiritual experience that really changes things; the in-depth type that brings you alive and keeps you alive every day all the way.
8. Live your life and forget your age.
9. Keep contact with spiritual re-creative power and you will always and forever keep the positive principle going.